Old Testament Quotations in the
Synoptic Gospels, and the
Two-Document Hypothesis

SOCIETY OF BIBLICAL LITERATURE
SEPTUAGINT AND COGNATE STUDIES SERIES

Series Editor
Leonard J. Greenspoon

Number 37

Old Testament Quotations in the
Synoptic Gospels, and the
Two-Document Hypothesis

by
David S. New

Old Testament Quotations in the Synoptic Gospels, and the Two-Document Hypothesis

by
David S. New

Scholars Press
Atlanta, Georgia

Old Testament Quotations in the
Synoptic Gospels, and the
Two-Document Hypothesis

by
David S. New

Library of Congress Cataloging-in-Publication Data
New, David S.
  Old Testament quotations in the Synoptic Gospels, and the two-document
hypothesis / by David S. New.
    p. cm. — (Septuagint and cognate studies series ; no. 37)
    Includes bibliographical references and indexes.
    ISBN 1-55540-920-2 (alk. paper). — ISBN 1-55540-921-0 (pbk. : alk. paper)
    1. Two source hypotheses (Synoptics criticism) 2. Griesbach hypotheses
(Synoptics criticism) 3. Bible. O.T.—Quotations in the New Testament.   I. Title.
II. Series.
BS2555.2..N482   1993
226'.066—dc20   93-36734
                                                                 CIP

Printed in the United States of America
on acid-free paper

Table of Contents

Acknowledgements

I want to take this opportunity to express my sincere thanks and appreciation to those individuals who have helped make this publication possible.

This work is an extensively revised version of my doctoral dissertation, submitted to McMaster University in 1990. Stephen R. Westerholm not only was my thesis advisor, but he volunteered to read and criticize several drafts beyond that point. Thank-you, Steve, for all your hours of hard work, your valuable comments, the example of your scholarship, and your friendly support.

Thank-you, Claude E. Cox, for all you have done. Your assistance in many phases of this work was invaluable, and your advice and suggestions were always appreciated. It is no exaggeration to say that, without your efforts, this work would not have been published.

Thank-you, Albert Pietersma, for so generously giving of your time to read my rough draft. Your comments were very helpful and the conversations I had with you most stimulating.

Finally, I want to thank Mike Lang and the friendly staff of the McMaster Divinity College.

Chapter I

Introduction

The Synoptic Problem and the Two-Document Hypothesis

It is easily observed that the three gospels, Matthew, Mark, and Luke, have a great amount of material in common; indeed, similarity among the three often extends to exact or nearly exact verbal agreement — hence, "synoptic gospels." At the same time, however, there are striking dissimilarities. Stated in simplest terms, the "synoptic problem" asks how we can account for the similarities as well as dissimilarities among the synoptic gospels.

For more than a century and a half the synoptic problem has been debated without a satisfactory solution. Nevertheless, the "two-document hypothesis" has appealed to the majority of twentieth-century New Testament scholars, to the degree that one part of the hypothesis, that Mark is the oldest of the three synoptics and was the principal source used by Matthew and Luke, has been commonly referred to as "the one absolutely assured result"[1] of synoptic research. The two-document hypothesis also proposes that Matthew and Luke shared a second source, denoted by "Q."

A landmark in the development of the two-document hypothesis was the 1863 work, *Die synoptischen Evangelien: Ihr Ursprung und*

---

[1] G. M. Styler, "The Priority of Mark," in C. F. D. Moule, *The Birth of the New Testament* (2nd ed.; San Francisco: Harper & Row, 1982) 285.

geschichtlicher Charakter , by Heinrich Julius Holtzmann.[1] As Bo Reicke so succinctly put it, this publication "secured the final victory of this hypothesis in Protestant Germany."[2] Indeed, William R. Farmer, in his challenge to the two-document hypothesis,[3] seems by the very layout of his historical analysis to key on Holtzmann as the arch-culprit.[4] Farmer sees Holtzmann's synthesis as "essentially programmatic" because until this time there was virtually no consensus concerning the order of writing of the synoptic gospels and their sources.[5]

Holtzmann is rather whimsically described by Stephen Neill as "a typical German professor of the late nineteenth century. Slow, ponderous in style, without a trace of humour and with no concessions to the possible weaknesses of his readers, he moves rather laboriously from point to point."[6] Indeed, historians of biblical criticism are as ready to laud Holtzmann for the sheer volume of his painstaking research as for the importance of his results.[7]

Holtzmann's real interest in determining the order of writing of the synoptic gospels is his concluding twenty-nine page *Lebensbild Jesu* . Indeed, it would not be inaccurate to depict Holtzmann's quest as an assault on the bastion built by Strauss and the Tübingen school. Instead of the gospels providing only a reflection of the conflicts and tendencies of the early church as they did for the Tübingen school, they provide a source of

---

[1]Leipzig: Engelmann. In this early work Holtzmann posited a source (*Urmarcus* , which he designated "A") behind Mark. He later discarded this source (*Lehrbuch der historisch-kritischen Einleitung in das Neue Testament* [3rd ed.; Freiburg: J. C. B. Mohr, 1892] 351–353, 537).

[2]*The Roots of the Synoptic Gospels* (Philadelphia: Fortress, 1986) 5.

[3]*The Synoptic Problem: A Critical Analysis* (New York: Macmillan, 1964; 2nd ed., Dillsboro, North Carolina: Western North Carolina Press, 1976).

[4] Farmer entitles his first two chapters, "The Essential Developments in the Pre-Holtzmann Period" and "The Holtzmannian Synthesis," respectively, and then proceeds in the remainder of his history to show how this synthesis was adopted by the scholarly community.

[5]*The Synoptic Problem* , 36.

[6]*The Interpretation of the New Testament, 1861–1961* (London: Oxford University Press, 1964) 110.

[7]To cite only one example from the many: Werner Georg Kümmel, *The New Testament: The History of the Investigation of Its Problems* (Nashville: Abingdon, 1972) 151. Ben F. Meyer, on the other hand, in what is perhaps a back-handed but witty compliment, disparages "the transition from Strauss to Holtzmann ... as a passing from ill-starred genius to professorial industry" (*The Aims of Jesus* [London: SCM, 1979] 37).

historical information almost a century closer to the actual events of Jesus' life than that school had supposed. Whether one sees Holtzmann as a leader of those "liberals" who "searched the New Testament for a reflection of their own idea of religion as interior experience and ethical ideal",[1] or as a "conservative" who sought to preserve the historicity of the gospels against the extreme views of F. C. Baur and company,[2] it is clear that through Holtzmann's work the solution of the synoptic problem, the order of the writing of the three synoptic gospels, became an issue of prime importance, even if only as the servant of larger theological controversies.[3] Holtzmann's presupposition was that the earlier the source the more accurate the historical evidence it would provide. According to Ben F. Meyer, it was this "simplistic equation of 'early sources' with guileless history that led ... to the exaggeration of the importance of the synoptic problem"; in fact, Meyer argues, the chronological order of the synoptic gospels does not in itself determine which of the traditions was the oldest.[4] One of those who have recently opposed the two-document hypothesis, Bernard Orchard, claims that not only did the Griesbach hypothesis (that the order of dependence was Matthew, Luke, Mark) virtually disappear because it became identified with the passing theology of the Tübingen school, but that the two-document hypothesis became identified with the concept of the historicity of the gospel tradition.[5] We are now aware of the weakness of Holtzmann's presupposition linking order of dependence of the gospels with historical accuracy. Hence, if Orchard's claim that the two-document hypothesis gained scholarly acceptance on the coattails of a larger theological debate concerning historicity of the gospels is correct, the time has come to re-examine the grounds of the two-document hypothesis.

---

[1]Meyer, *Aims* , 36.

[2]Bernard Orchard, *Matthew, Luke & Mark* (Manchester: Koinonia, 1976) 7.

[3]Holtzmann himself, as he stated in the opening paragraph of his 1863 work, was quite aware that this work would impress many theological readers as an exercise in ingenuity of doubtful worth, and so went on to claim that this is the only way to initiate the debate on the history of Jesus' time (*Die synoptischen Evangelien* , 1).

[4]*Aims* , 38.

[5]*Matthew* , 7.

Contemporary Scholarship on the Two-document Hypothesis

In recent years the two-document hypothesis has been challenged, particularly in the person of William R. Farmer, who fired his first shot with the amusingly titled article, "A 'Skeleton in the Closet' of Gospel Research",[1] and followed it up with the monograph, *The Synoptic Problem: A Critical Analysis* . Consequent to these publications, the synoptic problem, and the two-document hypothesis in particular, is once again a current issue in the scholarly literature. A hasty survey of monographs published in the last few years yields as examples: *The Two-Source Hypothesis: A Critical Appraisal* ,[2] *The Roots of the Synoptic Gospels,* [3] and *The Order of the Synoptics: Why Three Synoptic Gospels?* .[4] Several seminars and colloquia have been held over the past two decades involving scholars from around the globe:[5] since 1966 the Society of Biblical Literature has fostered continuous research on the synoptic problem; starting in 1971 and continuing for several years, the Society of New Testament Studies did likewise; 1970 witnessed the Pittsburgh Festival of the Gospels held at Pittsburgh Theological Seminary; the Johann Jakob Griesbach Bicentenary Colloquium, 1776-1976, was held at Münster (Westphalia) in 1976;[6] the Colloquy on the Relationships Among the Gospels at San Antonio in 1977; the Cambridge Conference on the Synoptic Gospels in 1979;[7] the international symposium at Jerusalem in 1984.

If we no longer seek to know the order of the writing of the synoptic gospels in order to determine which gospel would give best access to the history of Jesus' time, why should present scholarship interest itself in the

---

[1]*Biblical Research* 6 (1961) 18–42.

[2]Arthur J. Bellinzoni, Jr., Joseph B. Tyson, William O. Walker, Jr., ed. (Macon, Georgia: Mercer University Press, 1985).

[3]Bo Reicke (Philadelphia: Fortress, 1986).

[4]Bernard Orchard, Harold Riley (Macon, Georgia: Mercer University Press, 1987).

[5]For details on seminars, conferences, and colloquia previous to 1983, including lists of participants, see William R. Farmer, ed., *New Synoptic Studies: The Cambridge Gospel Conference and Beyond* (Macon, Georgia: Mercer University Press, 1983) vii–xxiii.

[6]For papers presented here, see Bernard Orchard and Thomas R. W. Longstaff, ed., *J. J. Griesbach: Synoptic and Text-critical Studies, 1776–1976* (Cambridge: Cambridge University Press, 1978).

[7]For papers presented here, see Farmer, ed., *New Synoptic Studies* .

synoptic problem, other than the straightforward desire to satisfy intellectual curiosity and resolve an issue that has a long pedigree?

One reason a solution to the synoptic problem is desirable is that inasmuch as the gospels provide a window onto the life of the early church, according to the tenets of form criticism, a determination of the order of their dependence would help to elucidate that history. If one gospel writer, for example, used another gospel as a source, his church may have had contact with that of the other gospel's writer. Also, theological concepts peculiar to the writer of the second gospel may have been of particular interest to his church. These examples can easily be multiplied.

A second reason for interest in the two-document hypothesis is that it served as a springboard for form criticism, as found in the works of Dibelius and Bultmann. As Joseph A. Fitzmyer observes:

> I am, however, aware that [form criticism is not] ... organically or necessarily tied to the Two-Source Theory.... Yet, historically, it was applied to the Gospels on the basis of the Two-Source Theory, as the works of M. Dibelius and R. Bultmann manifest on almost every page. I know of no comparable Form Critical studies that operate on the basis of another theory and have commanded the attention of scholars which can claim to rival the Dibelius-Bultmann approach.[1]

The two-document hypothesis is used in the service of form criticism to illustrate those changes in pericopes which are thought to have taken place in the movement of the gospel from the early Palestinian church to the hellenistic church.

A third reason for a solution to the synoptic problem is that some solution of the synoptic problem, usually the two-document hypothesis, is generally assumed in redaction critical work.[2] Graham Stanton states the

---

[1] "The Priority of Mark and the 'Q' Source in Luke," in *Jesus and Man's Hope* , vol. 1 (Pittsburgh: Pittsburgh Theological Seminary, 1970) 133.

[2] To mention only two examples: D. E. Garland, *The Intention of Matthew 23* (Leiden: Brill, 1979); J. D. Kingsbury, *The Parables of Jesus in Matthew 13* (London, 1969).

case quite clearly: "If the Griesbach hypothesis ... were to be accepted, many of the conclusions accepted by most Matthean specialists would be falsified, for they rest on the presupposition that Matthew used two sources, Mark and Q."[1] In addition, if we did not know about Mark and Luke, we would find it very difficult to isolate Matthew's sources. This would mean that "redaction" critics would have a great deal of difficulty in distinguishing traditional material from its Matthean redaction. As Stanton remarks, "Most scholars would agree that the attempt to make sense of ... [a] gospel as it stands without recourse to source critical hypotheses is rather like trying to play a violin or cello with one's left hand tied behind one's back: rather limited results are still possible, but that is all that can be said!"[2]

A fourth reason for further work on the synoptic problem is that its solution is most taken for granted in textbooks, from which young minds get the impression that the problem has been forever resolved. This generates a whole new generation who perpetuate this myth. However, the situation is changing. As J. A. T. Robinson has observed, "The consensus frozen by the success of 'the fundamental solution' propounded by B. H. Streeter has begun to show signs of cracking. Though it is still the dominant hypothesis, incapsulated in the textbooks, its conclusions can no longer be taken for granted as among the 'assured results' of biblical criticism."[3]

A fifth reason for examining the status of the two-document hypothesis is that presuppositions concerning some solution of the synoptic problem can affect textual choices.[4]

Considering the importance of a solution to the synoptic problem for synoptic research, the recent challenge to the status of the two-document hypothesis and the increased interest in the synoptic problem are not inappropriate and none too early.

---

[1]"The Origin and Purpose of Matthew's Gospel: Matthean Scholarship from 1945 to 1980," in Wolfgang Haase, ed., *Aufstieg und Niedergang der romischen Welt* 2.25.3 (Berlin: Walter de Gruyter, 1985) 1899.

[2]Haase, *Austieg* , 1896.

[3]*Redating the New Testament* (London: SCM, 1976) 93.

[4] Gordon D. Fee, "Modern Text Criticism and the Synoptic Problem," in Orchard and Longstaff, ed., *J. J. Griesbach* , especially 161–169.

Need for a Re-examination of OT Quotations in the Synoptics

In his 1863 publication Holtzmann points to a solution of the synoptic problem. With some nuancing, he noted that all of Mark's citations from the Old Testament were from the Septuagint. On the other hand, Matthew's citations fell into two groups: *Contextcitate* , those in common with Mark and from the Septuagint, and *Reflexionscitate* , those not found in Mark and from the Hebrew text. Holtzmann then argued that Matthew shows a preference for the Hebrew text when on his own but used Mark (actually a proposed Urmarcus) as his cue to the Septuagint in other instances.

Despite the fact that Holtzmann is acclaimed the figure who set the two-document hypothesis firmly in stone, his argument based on Old Testament citations has not been the subject of systematic study. Even Burnett Hillman Streeter's monumental and comprehensive work, *The Four Gospels: A Study of Origins* ,[1] which for more than a generation served to close the book on the synoptic problem in its presentation of the decisive solution, makes no mention of this argument.

I propose, therefore, on the suggestion of Holtzmann's argument, to examine the OT quotations in the synoptic gospels in order to determine if the variety of text-types exhibited fall into a pattern which supports either the two-document hypothesis or the Griesbach position. Discussion will be limited to these two theories because they are the two most prominent theories regarding the synoptic problem.

One of the first questions to be answered is whether or not Matthew's citations can be as neatly grouped as Holtzmann's argument would suggest. Recent scholarship (see chapter 3) has focused on the "fulfilment quotations" in Matthew, which somewhat parallel Holtzmann's *Reflexionscitate* , but there is no consensus with regard to the definition of this group. Can the group be clearly defined as a group vis-à-vis Matthew's other citations? Can it be shown, for example, that all of these quotations have a common text-form, that they all come from a specific OT source or are handled in the same fashion by the evangelist? If so, and if it can also be

---

[1] London: Macmillan, 1924.

demonstrated that the citations shared by Mark and Matthew are all of a text-type different from that shown in quotations unique to Matthew, this might suggest Matthew's dependence on Mark for common quotations.

For quotations appearing in more than one gospel (which are dealt with in chapter 4), analyses will be made of the synoptic relationships for the individual quotations. Here the two-document and Griesbach hypotheses will be hypothetically assumed in turn to see which better explains the text of the quotation as it appears in the various gospels. For example, if Matthew clearly adapts his form of the quotation to the context of a narrative identical for Matthew and Mark, in such a way that Mark's alteration of the Matthean form of the quotation would make no sense, the two-document hypothesis would be favored for that quotation. Moreover, it is easy to see why a gospel writer might alter a quotation to conform it more closely to the Septuagint, whereas movement away from the Septuagint, unless grammatically conditioned by the gospel context of the quotation, is less likely. Hence, closer conforming to the Septuagint may indicate that the less exact quotation has been copied and altered. These are a few of the kinds of argument that can be used to support one hypothesis over the other for an individual quotation. However, it is dangerous to generalize here. These arguments must be applied to the unique situation of each quotation.

This research is limited to the analysis of explicit OT quotations and does not deal with mere allusions to OT passages. The reason for this is simply one of practicality. There are far too many allusions for their adequate study to be included here.

It is not always clear whether a text is an explicit quotation or an allusion. However, there are rough guidelines for distinguishing the two. A quotation will normally have an introductory formula indicating that the following text is a quotation. Should this formula be lacking, evidence that it is the intention of the writer to make an explicit quotation will suffice. This evidence could take the form of several words identical to an OT text. On the other hand, if the text has no more than a fleeting resemblance to a possible OT text, then even an introductory formula might not indicate a biblical quotation.

In Holtzmann's time there did not yet exist a reliable critical Greek text of the gospels or of the LXX. Today the existence of critical editions of Old and New Testament texts and the advantage of recent advances in our knowledge of the status of Old Testament texts in the first century, give an urgency to the need for a re-examination of the quotations. It has been remarked that Streeter's 1924 monumental work may have been the last comprehensive study which seriously related the two disciplines of textual and synoptic criticism.[1]

Not only has there been no comprehensive examination of the synoptic quotations utilizing these critical editions of the Old and New Testament texts, New Testament synoptic scholars have not adequately dealt with the fluidity of both Hebrew and Greek texts in the first century. Graham Stanton notes this deficiency; he quotes K. Stendahl:

> New data are about to allow new and better founded hypotheses about text forms available in the first century A.D. Such a promising yet unfinished state of affairs both hinders and helps further progress in the study of the Matthean quotations. It makes it more probable that readings found in Matthew could witness to text forms actually available in Greek, prior to Matthew. It makes the recourse to testimonies less compelling as an explanation of textual peculiarities.[2]

Stanton continues, in his own words: "The importance of this work for the student of Matthew's gospel can hardly be over-estimated. Yet even though Stendahl drew attention to these new advances in scholarly knowledge nearly twelve years ago, they have not yet been taken seriously in Matthean scholarship."

It is time to remedy this situation.

---

[1]Fee, "Modern Text Criticism," 154.
[2]"The Origin and Purpose," 1933.

Chapter II

Holtzmann's Argument

The Concept of an *Urmarcus*

To understand fully Holtzmann's argument from Old Testament citations we need to see it within the context of his 1863 work, *Die synoptischen Evangelien: Ihr Ursprung und geschichtlicher Charakter* .[1]

A major reason for doing so is to draw attention to one of Holtzmann's main sources for the synoptics, his "A" (*Urmarcus*) document. This source gets underplayed, at the same time that the priority of Mark is spotlighted, in standard histories of New Testament criticism. Werner Georg Kümmel, for example, writes, "[Holtzmann] demonstrated most convincingly ... that Mark's Gospel was a source of the two other Synoptics .... Holtzmann differentiated a source back of Mark (that he called 'A') and tried to prove that Mark had abbreviated this source by deleting the discourses it contained, but all this was not an essential part of his argument."[2] Stephen Neill writes, "Holtzmann has, of course, his own eccentricity, such as must be allowed learned men. He invents a wholly unnecessary document A .... But, when allowance has been made for one such aberrant hypothesis, with Holtzmann we are in the main on solid

---

[1]Leipzig: Englemann.
[2]*The New Testament: The History of the Investigation of Its Problems* (Nashville: Abingdon, 1972) 151.

ground. Mark is the original apostolic document."[1] Why, we must ask, would someone of the acclaim of Holtzmann make such a centerpiece of A (he devotes one of five major divisions of his book to "Quelle A"; another he devotes to "Quelle Λ," so that if we force his thesis into a "two-document" mould, Mark would not seem to be one of the two documents) if it is "not essential" (*qua* Kümmel) or "unnecessary" (*qua* Neill)?

Holtzmann, in his survey of previous scholarship on the synoptic problem, believed there was only one point of consensus: that the three synoptic gospels are all dependent upon one common *Grundschrift* or *ur*-gospel.[2] The concept of an *ur*-gospel allowed the agreements among the synoptic gospels to be explained by the three synoptic evangelists each using the same *ur*-gospel independently of one another, rather than, as an alternative explanation has it, copying one another. Holtzmann, in outlining the history of the synoptic problem, recognized this distinctive grouping of theories, placing them under the headings "Die Urevangeliumshypothese" and "Die Benutzungshypothese," respectively.[3]

There is narrative material found in both Matthew and Luke which is not in Mark and cannot be in the *logia* if this is regarded as simply a collection of sayings. Holtzmann gets around this difficulty by including it in his *Urmarcus* .

Holtzmann entitles another part of his history "Die Marcushypothese." It is the *Marcushypothese* which Holtzmann states in the preface to his book will be his aim to establish.[4] Nevertheless, just what Holtzmann means by "Marcushypothese" is not immediately clear.

Our quest for Holtzmann's definition of "Marcushypothese" comes up short in the section under this title. He rarely uses the word. Where he does, he lists some scholars who "mehr oder minder in dasselbe Fahrwasser der Marcushypothese lenkten ... ein." Here is represented a great diversity of

---

[1]*The Interpretation of the New Testament, 1861–1961* (London: Oxford University Press, 1964) 110–111.
[2]*Die synoptischen Evangelien* , 66.
[3]*Die synoptischen Evangelien* , 15–20.
[4]*Die synoptischen Evangelien* , xiv.

theories: Mark as a source for Matthew, Matthew and Mark as mutually dependent, Matthew and Mark using a common source.[1]

Holtzmann, in writing about Karl Lachmann, speaks of the priority of Mark "in diesem Sinne":

> Schon Lachmann hatte keineswegs in diesem Sinne für die Priorität des Marcus votirt, vielmehr kommt er auf einen ursprünglichen Kanon der evangelischen Geschichte hinaus, der besonders rein im Marcus erhalten wäre, während Matthäus und Lucas manches alterirt hätten.[2]

This suggests that for Holtzmann Marcan priority does not simply mean Mark is a source for the other two synoptics. Marcan priority could also mean priority in a non-temporal sense, that Mark is a more trustworthy witness to the *ur* -gospel than either Matthew or Luke. This is made more explicit when Holtzmann notes, "Besonders aber seit Ewald's Auftreten verstehen die Meisten unter der sogenannten Priorität des Marcus blos Dies, dass er im Verhältnisse zu den beiden Andern den ursprünglichsten Typus der Erzählung erkennen lasse."[3] This makes clear the meaning of "Marcushypothese." It means Marcan priority, but not simply in the sense in which we would speak of Marcan priority today. Instead, "Marcus hypothese" includes the theory that our Mark gives a better witness to the *ur* -gospel than the other two synoptics.

Holtzmann devotes several pages to the issue of whether it was an *Urmarcus* or our Mark that was a source for Matthew and Luke.[4] He shows how passages found only in Mark, and others found only in Matthew and

---

[1]That "Marcushypothese" can serve as an umbrella term to designate several theories is confirmed in Holtzmann, *Hand-commentar zum neuen Testament: Erster Band: Die Synoptiker* (2nd. ed.; Freiburg: Mohr, 1892), xv. Here, with the introductory clause, "Die Marcustheorie in ihren verschiedenen Formen ist vertreten in folgenden Werken," Holtzmann lists several works, among which is Weisse's 1838 publication in which Mark, rather than an *ur* -gospel, is posited as a source for Matthew and Luke, and Holtzmann's own 1863 book in which an *ur* -gospel serves as source for all three synoptics.

[2]*Die synoptischen Evangelien* , 58.

[3]*Die synoptischen Evangelien* , 59.

[4]*Die synoptischen Evangelien* , 58–64.

Luke against Mark, provide difficulties for those who would like to posit our
Mark as a source rather than an *Urmarcus* .[1]

Taking the example of such passages as his lead, Holtzmann
proceeds to elaborate five types of evidence he thinks demonstrate that our
canonical Mark must have been preceded by an *Urmarcus* .[2] (1) In some
places Mark abbreviates in such a way that the clarity of the narrative is
destroyed. (2) Some narratives are obviously more original in the form in
which they appear in Matthew, or in Mark contain more mythical elements.
(3) Mark often shortens speeches to the point where they lose continuity. (4)
Matthew and Luke use several words and expressions in common against
Mark. (5) Matthew and Luke often agree in formulae and sentences which
are left out, against Mark. Whether or not these cases are decisive is not at
issue here. What is important is that Holtzmann believes he has a strong case
against our Mark as source for the other two synoptics, and for an
Urmarcus. [3]

---

[1]*Die synoptischen Evangelien* , 59.
[2]*Die synoptischen Evangelien* , 60–63.
[3]While Holtzmann in *Die synoptischen Evangelien* definitely sees Mark as merely a good
witness to the *ur* -gospel but a document separate from it, he has adopted a different
position by the time his later works were published.

   An examination of Holtzmann's later works does little to resolve why he may
have changed his position. In his *Hand-Commentar* , in fact, Holtzmann does not center
his attention on the Mark versus *Urmarcus* issue. He uses phrases, here and there, which
indicate almost a neutrality: "Mc, resp. Urmc" (p. 4), "unser Mc, bzw., falls die
Urmchypothese Bestand haben soll" (p. 24). He relegates this issue to a mere point of
historical interest, noting that some scholars vote for an *Urmarcus* of varying likeness to
our Mark while others opt for the direct use of Mark by the other synoptics (p. 4).
Holtzmann often writes in such a way that one could easily read him to mean that Mark
was a source of Matthew and Luke; for example, in one of the only instances where he
seems to state a position on this issue:

> Die Forschungen, deren Ergebniss in diesen Sätzen niedergelegt ist, führten mit
> Nothwendigkeit auf eine Ansicht, derzufolge die synopt. Texte ihre gemeinsame
> Wurzel im Mc-Text besitzen, und daraus wieder entsprang die Vermuthung, dass
> der ursprüngliche Plan der evang. Geschichtserzählung sich noch in unserem 2.
> Evglm erhalten habe. (p. 6)

This could mean only that in Mark we have the best witness to an earlier *ur* -gospel, in the
non-temporal sense of Marcan priority.

   In all of this Holtzmann's main concern is to give an account of the history of
the tradition concerning Jesus' life. He gives greater emphasis to the role of the oral
tradition and the concerns and contributions of the early church in this book (especially pp.

Holtzmann characterizes Mark as, at minimum, leaving out much[1] of the Grundschrift which he labels "A."[2] He goes on to compare Mark with A, giving details of how the two differ.[3] His research proceeds along two lines: (1) to investigate the content and form of A; (2) to determine the relations of the synoptics. The latter is accomplished by a series of six critical studies: (1) the composition of Matthew, (2) the composition of Luke, (3) doublets, (4) Old Testament citations, (5) stylistic characteristics, (6) the different modifications of the original by the three synoptics. Holtzmann then claims that any of the above studies (*Hauptkriterien*) by itself can determine the relationship of the synoptic gospels.[4] In our case we shall examine Holtzmann's study of Old Testament citations.

Holtzmann's Argument

Having set forth in earlier chapters his solution of the synoptic problem, that Matthew, Mark, and Luke independently used a common source A, and that Matthew and Luke independently used a common source

---

13–22). In this way one might almost see here in Holtzmann a foreshadowing of later form and tradition criticism. He seems open to the question whether any common source of the synoptics was oral tradition, a written *ur* -gospel, or a combination of both in several layers (p. 3). He places great faith in Eusebius' witness to Papias (p. 9), which is why he sees Mark as best preserving the tradition concerning Jesus. Above all, Holtzmann here seems less concerned with the details of how the three synoptics came into being than with using what we can find in Mark as a mine of historical fact.

In Holtzmann's other later work, *Lehrbuch der historisch-kritischen Einleitung in das Neue Testament* (3rd ed.; Freiburg: Mohr, 1892), he states, in fine print, that he has changed his earlier position on several points (p. 350). One of these is that he now believes Luke has a copy of Matthew. Because of this the most important reason for differentiating between Mark and an *Urmarcus* disappears. He quickly and summarily disposes of the *ur* -gospel position in a manner of writing which hardly falls short of sarcasm (pp. 351–353). As one reason against an *Urmarcus* , vis-à-vis Mark itself as a source, Holtzmann asks how three evangelists could have known to arrange their material so that where one failed to follow the order of the original the other two would follow it faithfully. Holtzmann offers this point as a proposition in his new theory that Luke had access to Matthew, as well as Mark (although he does not make the connection here).

[1]*Die synoptischen Evangelien* , 103. In the following section, pp. 103–107, Holtzmann shows how the three synoptic gospels are modifications of the *ur* -gospel.

[2]*Die synoptischen Evangelien* , 66.

[3]*Die synoptischen Evangelien* , 107–113.

[4]*Die synoptischen Evangelien* , 67.

A, Holtzmann proceeded[1] to show how the form of the Old Testament quotations in the synoptic gospels can be explained[2] by his solution, but not by other attempted solutions, of the synoptic problem.

Holtzmann's contribution here is to relate previous scholarly discussions of the OT quotations to the synoptic problem and show how his

---

[1]*Die synoptischen Evangelien* , 258–264. Evidence as to just how unknown is Holtzmann's treatment of Old Testament citations in *Die synoptischen Evangelien* can be found in comments in the recent literature on the term *Reflexionscitate* , used in Holtzmann's treatment. Even in such a thoroughly documented study specifically on a group of such citations as George M. Soares Prabhu's *The Formula Quotations in the Infancy Narrative of Matthew: An Inquiry into the Tradition History of Mt 1–2* (Rome: Biblical Institute Press, 1976) we read, "The earliest explicit mention of *Reflexionszitat* that we know of occurs in Holtzmann's *Hand-Commentar* (1892)" (p. 20). Soares Prabhu cites works going back to 1713 and, commenting on what is seemingly a leave-no-stone-unturned search, in a labyrinthine footnote rues the fact that he was unable to obtain an 1871 work which was quoted in another work of 1877 which may have implied the existence of the term. Raymond E. Brown is also caught remiss here. He observes in a footnote that "the German term *Reflexionszitate* ... appears as early as the 1889 edition of H. J. Holtzmann's commentary on the synoptics" (*The Birth of the Messiah: A Commentary on the Infancy Narratives in Matthew and Luke* [London: Geoffrey Chapman, 1977] 96, n.1). True, his "as early as" does not commit him to the denial of earlier references, but it is interesting that his chapter bibliography includes F. van Segbroeck, "Les citations d'accomplissement dans l'évangile selon Matthieu d'après trois ouvrages récents," in M. Didier, ed., *L'Évangile selon Matthieu: Rédaction et théologie* (Gembloux: J. Duculot, 1972) pp.107–130, in which can be found reference (p. 109, n.12) to *Reflexionscitate* and the same 1889 edition of Holtzmann's commentary. All of which would indicate an unawareness of a more detailed account by the same scholar using the same term some generation earlier, especially since footnote references have a habit of longevity in the scholarly community, once set loose in the literature.

[2]Holtzmann begins his discussion of Old Testament citations by stating that they provide very important material for judging the relationship of the synoptics. This discussion constitutes a section of a large chapter entitled "Proben." This might suggest that the sections of the chapter provide proofs for the validity of Holtzmann's form of the two-document hypothesis. It could also mean that each section furnishes an experiment, a test, an example, or a check which, if the experiment goes the way the experimenter hopes it will, will provide further confirmation in the direction of a positive proof; Holtzmann does use the term *Hauptkriterien* which would suggest that an examination of Old Testament citations could provide a criterion or test to confirm or deny some hypothesis, but which would not by itself fully prove the hypothesis. Holtzmann does not make any categorical statement that he claims to be giving a sufficient proof. At the end of the first paragraph of his discussion he says that he will present his results without examining in detail all the individual citations. This is not what one would expect if a complete and sufficient proof or argument were intended. Holtzmann, then, is offering his discussion of the OT citations, not as a sufficient proof of his solution to the synoptic problem, but as confirmation of his solution.

Perhaps the fact that Holtzmann offers his analysis of OT quotations as confirmation, rather than proof, might help to explain why his discussion of OT citations in relation to the two-document hypothesis has gone unnoticed in the scholarly literature on the subject.

solution to the synoptic problem can explain difficulties discussed in earlier examinations of the quotations.

He makes special reference to two notable examinations of the quotations, those of Carl August Credner and Friedrich Bleek. The former concluded that Matthew quoted freely from a Septuagint (LXX) text, but one which, in the case of certain messianic passages, had been compared with, and altered towards, the *Urtext* (MT). Holtzmann agreed with Bleek's view that those citations in Matthew which occurred "mitten im Context der Erzählung" originated in the LXX, while those which "aus der eigenen Reflexion des Evangelisten stammenden" came from the *Grundtext* (MT).[1] Citing other scholars, Holtzmann notes that the exception is Matt 1:23, which belongs to the evangelist but comes from the LXX.

Holtzmann applies Bleek's observations to the synoptic problem by claiming that those citations in Matthew which occurred "mitten im Context der Erzählung" not only originate in the LXX, but do so precisely because Matthew finds them in his A source, a source "in welcher allein der Grundsatz, nach LXX zu citiren, streng durchgeführt war."[2] On the other hand, those citations in Matthew which "aus der eigenen Reflexion des Evangelisten stammenden" came from the *Grundtext* (MT) because, while Matthew was a Jew who was familiar with, and equally fluent in, both the Hebrew and Greek versions of the OT, he nevertheless preferred the Hebrew text when quoting the OT on his own.

Holtzmann begins his analysis by listing the ten OT citations which are found only in Matthew, and into which his characteristic formula, ἵνα πληρωθῇ, is inserted: 1:23 (Isa 7:14–16); 2:15 (Hos 11:1), 18 (Jer 31:15),

---

[1]Bleek (*Beiträge zur Einleitung und Auslegung der heiligen Schrift. I. Beiträge zur Evangelien-kritik* [Berlin: G. Reimer, 1846] 56–59) differentiated between two groups of Old Testament citations: (1) fulfilment (*Erfüllung*) citations in which Matthew presents his own idea of what event fulfils what citation and then translates from the Hebrew even where it differs from the LXX in wording and meaning; (2) the occasional reference to or use of Old Testament citations on the lips of characters found in a narrative, in which Matthew uses the LXX sometimes verbatim and sometimes freely, with the possible exception of 11:10 and 26:31, where the Hebrew may have been considered. Bleek considered Matthew an educated Jew who wrote in Greek, knew the LXX and MT, and used one or more Greek gospels in which were Old Testament citations of the second type.
[2]*Die synoptischen Evangelien* , 261.

23 (Isa 11:1); 4:15–16 (Isa 8:23; 9:1); 8:17 (Isa 53:4); 12:17–21 (Isa 42:1–3); 13:35 (Ps 87:2); 21:5 (Zech 9:9); 27:9 (Zech 11:12).

Of the above, 2:15 and 2:23 correspond accurately to the Hebrew (*Urtext*), which in this case has a different meaning than the LXX. Matt 27:9 renders the Hebrew very freely, but without any suggestion of the LXX. One citation, 1:23, predominantly agrees with the LXX, because only in this form, Holtzmann argues, does Isa 7:14 have a messianic sense. The rest of the above citations are based on the Hebrew text, "doch so, dass der Ausdruck der LXX Einfluss übt." For example, the first half of 13:35 agrees with the LXX, while the second half agrees with the Hebrew.

Holtzmann believes that whenever Matthew adds to the tradition his own OT quotations, as opposed to those he finds in A or some other gospel source, he shows influence of the Hebrew. On this basis he concludes that Matthew preferred the Hebrew text, with the one exception (Isa 7:14) for which he had a definite motive for departing from the Hebrew.

Holtzmann goes directly into a discussion of the *Contextcitate* without, unfortunately, first defining *Contextcitat* . That he prefaces the term with "sogenannten" suggests that the expression is not his, but one current in contemporary scholarship. Again, since Holtzmann does cite Bleek and credit him with the correct classification, we shall assume that this is whence he takes his definitions. In contrast to what we have assumed Holtzmann would call the *Reflexionscitate* (those introduced by the narrator), the *Contextcitate* appear in the context of the narrative on the lips of a character.

Holtzmann notes that the *Contextcitate* in Matthew bear clear witness in most cases to the LXX. However, there are exceptions, and these are such "dass nur die Annahme einer Quelle im Sinn von A, nicht aber ... die Marcushypothese den Schlüssel zum vollen Verständnisse der Sachlage bietet."[1] First Holtzmann notes that there are seventeen citations which Matthew and Mark have in common; these would have been taken from A. Ten of these agree verbally. Four contain "nur unbedeutende Variationen": Mark 7:10 = Matt 15:4; Mark 10:7–8 = Matt 19:5; Mark 12:29–30 = Matt 22:37; Mark 15:34 = Matt 27:46. In these cases Matthew often follows the

---

[1]Here "Marcushypothese" has the narrow sense, the theory that Mark (the text we have today) was the source for Matthew and Luke.

LXX even where it differs from the Hebrew text. In two passages, Mark 4:12 = Matt 13:14–15; Mark 10:19 = Matt 19:18–19, Matthew follows the LXX more closely than Mark. Here Matthew has clearly followed A more accurately than Mark. Holtzmann reminds us of Mark's propensity to abbreviate. He also notes that Matt 19:19b, which refers to Lev 19:18, and the τῆς ποίμνης found in Matt 26:31 but not in the parallel Mark 14:27, are added by Matthew.

The final citation of the seventeen common to Matthew and Mark, Matt 22:24, presents a case where Matthew illustrates his preference for the Hebrew to such an extent that he modified the text found in A. Evidence for this is the influence of the Hebrew text found in the word ἐπιγαμβρεύσεις, which is missing in the parallel Mark 12:19. Holtzmann claims the word was also missing from A. Matthew took an allusion (as found in A) to Deut 25:5, and gave it the form of a direct citation.

Holtzmann then notes that the citations in the narrative on Jesus' temptation are from the LXX with slight modification. These citations are found only in Matthew and Luke, not in Mark. The narrative found in Mark abbreviates A.[1] That Matthew and Luke derived the quotations from A is clear from their Septuagintal form.

The quotations in Matt 22:32, 37[2] and their parallels in Mark present a problem. Holtzmann's theory would suggest that the source of these quotations must be A, and that, therefore, they must be based on the LXX. However, some scholars previous to Holtzmann had argued that they are based on the Hebrew, not the LXX. Here Holtzmann notes Ritschl's observation that v. 32 corresponds to LXX[A] and v. 37 corresponds more closely to a variant reading in the LXX than to the Hebrew. He also counters the notion that Matt 3:3 is a *Reflexion* of Matthew by pointing out that all three synoptics have this citation, and therefore it is found in A; appropriately, it is Septuagintal.

---

[1]Mark adds ἦν μετὰ τῶν θηρίων. Holtzmann claims this could not have been in A or Matthew and Luke would not have overlooked it. This confirms his position that all three synoptic gospels use a common source, in opposition to the *Marcushypothese* which posits our Mark as a source for the other two synoptics (*Die synoptischen Evangelien* , 69–70).

[2]Holtzmann mistakenly refers to v. 31 here, meaning v. 32.

The next major issue Holtzmann examines concerns those *Contextcitate* in Matthew which do not come from the LXX. For these citations, he argues, Matthew is totally independent of A. In this group belongs "das Contextcitat der Vorgeschichte," Matt 2:6 (= Mic 5:1). While here some influence may be conceded to a Greek text like that of LXX^A, the predominant witness is to the Hebrew text. Holtzmann claims that, unlike Bleek's theory which is unable to explain a citation which appears in the context of a narrative and is from the Hebrew, his theory can. His explanation is that Matthew himself created the *Vorgeschichte* in which the citation is situated.

Holtzmann mentions a few more *Contextcitate* which do not come from the LXX, and are, therefore, not from A. The citations of the Sermon of the Mount, Matt 5:31, 33, bear witness neither to the LXX nor to the Hebrew text. This is because they come from a secondary Matthean source.[1] From this source as well comes Matt 5:4, which witnesses to LXX Ps 37:11.

As Holtzmann sees it, in only one passage in Mark does the OT quotation not come from the LXX, and hence from A: Mark 1:2 (= Mal 3:1). The citation of Mark 1:2, formed according to the Hebrew, is also found in Matt 11:10 = Luke 7:27. In the case of Matthew and Luke, Holtzmann believes the citation is taken from Λ; but how can the presence in Mark (who otherwise finds his citations in A, although he may abbreviate these at times) of a citation based, not on the LXX, but on the Hebrew, be explained? Unless it can be shown how Mark derived the citation from a source other than A, the view that A derives quotations exclusively from the LXX is invalidated.

Holtzmann begins by noting that contemporary scholarship had suggested treating Mark 1:2, 3[2] as a parenthetical expression. Holtzmann suggests v. 3 was an insertion or marginal gloss found in A. Thus A read, "The beginning of the gospel of Jesus Christ, the Son of God. (As is written

---

[1]This source which is used among the synoptics by Matthew alone, especially in chapters. 5 and 23, is described by Holtzmann, *Die synoptischen Evangelien* , 162–163.

[2]Holtzmann says vv. 3, 4, but he must have meant vv. 2, 3, as he writes, "das ὡς γέγραπται als Parenthese zu nehmen, und ἀρχή mit ἐγένετο zu verbinden."

in the prophet Isaiah, 'Behold the voice of one crying in the wilderness, "Prepare the way of the Lord, make straight his paths."') John the baptizer appeared in the wilderness." This avoids the difficulty of having A present a citation by another prophet under the name of Isaiah, as would be the case if A were identical to Mark. But the quotation from Malachi (which Matthew and Luke had taken from source Λ) came to be seen as describing the mission of John the baptizer. This led Mark to insert it between the citation formula in A, which introduces Isaiah as the speaker, and the actual citation from Isaiah.[1] Since Mark left the citation formula intact, the result was the anomaly of a quotation from Malachi preceded by a citation formula referring to Isaiah.

The next case Holtzmann examines is that of the double occurrence (Matt 9:13; 12:7) of a citation from Hos 6:6, ἔλεος θέλω καὶ οὐ θυσίαν. This comes from the LXX, he claims, because there חֶסֶד is usually translated as ἔλεος. Because it comes from the LXX, we might next assume that it is a part of A which both Mark and Luke ignored. The two separated contexts in which the citation appears in Matthew (9:9–17; 12:1–8) are parallel with two consecutive passages in Mark (2:13–22, 23–28), suggesting that the citation may have been located in A in the area which is parallel to this part of Mark. On the other hand, Holtzmann notes that in both locations in Matthew the citation appears to be an insert: at 12:7 it does not form a coherent whole with the preceding two verses; at 9:13 it falls between a universal maxim and its application. That Matthew uses γάρ in 9:13 and 12:8 does not conceal the fact that there is no real logical connection here. Holtzmann concludes that Matthew in both cases took the Septuagintal citation of Hos 6:6 from the margin of A (= Mark 2:13–28) and worked it into both pericopes of this larger passage in such a way that at Matt 12:7 it referred back to its other use at Matt 9:13, making of the latter an instruction which was not followed.

Holtzmann offers a few characterizing remarks on each of the three evangelists. He claims that Matthew regularly abbreviates or omits parts of A

---

[1]One wonders where Holtzmann supposes Mark got this tradition that the Malachi citation was connected with John the baptizer, especially when he insists Mark had only one source, A (*Die synoptischen Evangelien* , 163).

when introducing citations of his own. As examples, 8:16–17; 12:17–21; 13:35; and 21:5 are cited.

In Luke, with the single exception 7:27 = Matt 11:10 = Mark 1:2, which is from the Hebrew, all citations are from the LXX. Usually, when Luke cites the Old Testament, he uses A. Here, however, he uses Λ, in which citations are from both the Hebrew text and the LXX.

When Mark's quotations differ from those of the other gospels, he "blos gedächtnissmässige Abweichungen bietet." Most of Mark's citations occur "im Context," that is, on the lips of the characters in the narrative. Only in the introductory passage is this not the case. Because Mark 15:28 is copied from Luke 22:37 and almost without exception deleted by contemporary critical authorities, Mark 1:3 presents the single *Reflexionscitat* found in A.

Holtzmann concludes his discussion of OT citations by listing other citations and allusions to OT passages found in Mark and, hence, in A. These are as follows: (1) explicit quotations: 7:6, 7, 10; 11:17; 12:10, 36; 14:27; (2) less clearly defined quotations: 2:25–26; 12:19, 26; (3) references to the OT: 1:44; 13:24; 15:34; (4) allusions (although some are allusions only because Mark has suppressed the quotation: 4:12; 9:44, 46, 48, 49; 10:3, 6, 7, 19; 12:29–31; 13:14).[1]

In summary, source A, in which all OT quotations are Septuagintal, provides all the OT quotations found in Mark (apart from 1:2), all the OT quotations found in Luke (except 7:27, which is from Λ, and perhaps 10:27), and many of the OT quotations found in Matthew. With the exception of a few OT quotations which come from other sources, those OT quotations in Matthew which are not from A, Matthew selects himself, preferring the Hebrew over the LXX.

---

[1]The final list we present here, separate from the other four because, as Holtzmann disparagingly remarks, "Dass aber in ebenso bewusster Weise auch ... [the list] auf das Alte Testament hingezielt sei, ist Privatdogma der Wilke'schen Kritik geblieben." The list (we have retained Holtzmann's "ff.," rather than assume it means "the following two verses") is: 1:12; 3:13ff, 20–21; 6:17ff; 7:24ff; 8:11ff; 9:2ff., 14ff; 11:1ff; 14:26ff; 15:1ff. It seems strange that 14:26ff is included in this list, seeing that 14:27 made Holtzmann's "ausgesprochene Citate" list.

Chapter III

Grouping Citations in the Synoptics by Text-Type

No effort of modern scholarship has pursued Holtzmann's lead in systematically examining Old Testament citations with respect to the synoptic problem. Nevertheless, because Holtzmann's argument relies on a distinct grouping of these citations, it will be helpful to consider a few of the more influential and recent studies of Old Testament citations in the synoptic gospels in order to clarify the issues regarding classifying the citations into groups.[1]

Krister Stendahl

Stendahl's book, *The School of St. Matthew and its Use of the Old Testament*,[2] was first published in 1954. A second edition of 1968 left the body of the work unchanged but added a preface.[3] In this preface Stendahl

---

[1]The works I have chosen to discuss are major monographs on the subject. Would that for our task of bringing together two vast and separate areas in the literature, that of the synoptic problem and that of Old Testament citations in the synoptics, we might use the ingenious method of one of Charles Dickens' characters who "wrote learnedly on 'Chinese metaphysics' by consulting an encyclopaedia under 'Chinese' and then under 'Metaphysics'." (For this amusing excursus into methodology, although his referents were different, I am indebted to George M. Soares Prabhu, *The Formula Quotations in the Infancy Narrative of Matthew: An Enquiry into the Tradition History of Mt 1–2* [Rome: Biblical Institute Press, 1976], 1).

[2]Lund: C. W. K. Gleerup.

[3]Here Stendahl suggests that Matthew was a Jew living in a Hellenistic Christian community composed of Jews and gentiles, which had made the transition to an

remarks that in spite of the prominence given in the title to a school, the "primary justification" for his study was the analysis of the OT text in the gospel. Indeed, the original work grew out of Stendahl's early involvement with the study of the Qumran texts.

Stendahl begins his examination of the quotations by defining a few terms.[1] In decided understatement he observes, "The question of where to draw the line between quotations and allusions is a problem in itself." Stendahl tries to avoid this difficulty by restricting his investigation to those passages introduced by a formula and those which, although lacking a formula, are conscious quotations, judging from the context, or which agree verbatim with some passage in the LXX or MT.

Stendahl also begins with the conception of two general groups of quotations. Matthean quotations with parallels in one or more of the other synoptics are said to have a fairly pure LXX text. Contrasted with this group are the "formula quotations" (the same quotations as those referred to in German as *Reflexionscitate*), none of which has a synoptic parallel. The eleven formula quotations (Matt 1:23; 2:6; 2:15; 2:18; 2:23; 4:15–16; 8:17; 12:18–21; 13:35; 21:5; 27:9–10) have a text form which differs noticeably from the LXX.

Instead of positing some unknown text as source for these quotations, Stendahl declares that what we have here is a different "citation technique" from that found in the quotations having parallels with other synoptics.[2] While dependence on the MT is greater in the formula quotations, this is insufficient to explain fully the Matthean form of these

---

increasingly gentile constituency without suffering the usual tension and problems. Matthew's community stood in sharp contrast to the local Jewish community, but lacked the internal friction so common to other contemporary Christian communities of mixed ethnic backgrounds. Hence, Jewish traditions which in other communities would be suspect, here could be preserved and elaborated.

Stendahl's major reservation about his first edition is that the explosion in findings at Qumran makes it "clear that a wider variety [of OT text types] — actually demonstrated and reasonably projected — minimizes to some extent the degree of textual creativity which this study assigns to 'the School of St. Matthew'" (*School* , vi). Nevertheless, he notes that some explanation for the peculiar text form of the Matthean formula quotations must still be sought.

[1]*School* , 45–46.
[2]*School* , 126–127.

quotations. Stendahl rules out the possibility that Matthew was simply correcting the LXX to greater agreement with the MT, or that Matthew used the MT but was consciously or unconsciously influenced by the LXX. Signs of an Aramaic version which was then nuanced with the LXX find little support in agreement with known Targum texts. Stendahl concludes that Matthew wrote in Greek and selected freely from several OT traditions and methods of interpretation, in a process Stendahl calls "targumizing."[1]

A third group of quotations, peculiar to Matthew but without the fulfilment formula, and occurring in some instances in a synoptic context, Stendahl finds dependent on the LXX.

Stendahl observes a very close agreement between Matthew and Mark in common quotations. Luke tends to deviate more from the LXX, but this is only in form, in order better to merge his quotations with their context. The material common to Matthew and Luke shows fewer survivals of Semitic form than the Marcan quotations, and tends to be in the form of allusions rather than quotations, with clear dependence on the LXX. Material peculiar to Luke is even more Septuagintal, but it is mostly in the form of allusions. This suggests that Q and other material common to Matthew and Luke were formed in "a consciously LXX milieu" and that Semitic indicators do not point to a tradition of Semitic quotations, but merely present surviving remnants.[2]

It would give a clear picture of Matthew's quotation technique if all his quotations in common with other synoptics were based on the LXX, and all the rest deviated from the LXX in striking fashion. Unfortunately the real situation is far more complex. Matthew's formula quotations show familiarity with the LXX, and his peculiar but non-formula quotations are sometimes pure LXX. Add to this the fact that Matthew's genealogy of Jesus is Septuagintal in the forms of its names and in its allusions, and the fact that

---

[1] Here Stendahl raises a question that his later solution of a school seems inadequate to answer. He asks how the texts of Matthew's formula quotations could claim the authority they must have had to be useful, considering that the Targums did not obtain authority in Judaism (*School*, 127).

[2] Here Stendahl realizes that his observations are at odds with what we would expect in Q. If Q is the same as Papias' *Logia*, one would expect it to be Semitic. Instead, Stendahl finds that "precisely those quotations which consist of the words of Jesus are most clearly LXX in their nature" (*School*, 150).

Matthew often adapts Marcan quotations to the LXX, and the fact that in the
Psalm texts familiar through the liturgy the LXX is given purest witness, and
Stendahl feels compelled to conclude that Matthew's gospel developed in a
church milieu in which the Bible was the LXX.[1] On the other hand, some of
the formula quotations would not have made sense in their context in
Septuagintal form.

Stendahl asserts that "most of the quotations in the gospels have
given us the impression of a conscious desire to reproduce the LXX text
correctly."[2] He also declares that this is "the impression" made by the NT in
general. This, he argues, "gives us reason not to resort to the explanation of
'free quoting from memory' as soon as any differences appear." He has in
mind, of course, the formula quotations, to which we cannot locate the
Vorlage . In other words, Stendahl wants all quotations to be accepted as
appearing in the form in which they were intended. If they deviate from the
OT text, they were meant to deviate. "The intention to quote literally, and the
practice of checking the text with the Greek text available may be taken for
granted in the synoptic material. The deviations in Luke are due to his desire
to write good literature."[3]

Stendahl claims that the formula quotations were part of the final
stage of redaction and the quotations in common with other synoptics came
from Mark and Q. It is in this vein that Stendahl writes, "This process of
making the quotations conform to the LXX was a very early one, as can be
seen from the fact that it is in the words of Jesus that we find the LXX
character to be most consistent."[4]

Stendahl is convinced that the quotations common to two or more
synoptics, especially those from Isaiah and the Minor Prophets, used a
recension closer to LXX^A than LXX^B.[5] Quotations from Psalms are in
closer agreement with LXX^B. Each book of the LXX must be examined

---

[1]*School* , 150–151.
[2]*School* , 158.
[3]*School* , 163–164.
[4]*School* , 162.
[5]*School* , 174.

separately. By noting manuscript variation in the LXX, the gap between the OT quotations in the synoptics and the LXX is diminished.

Stendahl asserts that Matthew did not use nor know another Greek version of the OT, even of the type discovered by D. Barthélemy in the Wilderness of Judaea in 1952. Barthélemy had suggested that these fragments of Micah, Jonah, Nahum, Habakkuk, Zephaniah, and Zechariah, dated at the end of the first century of our era, were from a Septuagintal text corrected to a greater agreement with the MT. Stendahl notes that variations from the LXX in the formula quotations are of various kinds, and are unlikely to be explained by adherence to a single text. In addition, the variants within LXX manuscripts cannot explain the very marked differences offered by the formula quotations.

As argument against a single *Vorlage* behind the formula quotations Stendahl attempts to demonstrate the similarity between Matthew's formula quotations and one of the scrolls discovered at Qumran, the Habakkuk Commentary (DSH).[1] Just as in Matthew the quotations are interpreted as fulfilled by the words or deeds of Jesus, so in DSH the first two chapters of Habakkuk are applied to the Teacher of Righteousness. The references to Habakkuk are introduced by a formula which Stendahl sees as functioning in the same way as the fulfilment formula in Matthew. Stendahl claims that while DSH falls generally under the genre *midrash* , it is so exclusively carried out from the viewpoint of the sect that it is more than simply a commentary, it is what Stendahl prefers to designate *midrash pesher* .

The text of DSH varies considerably from the MT, but mostly in such a way that it forms an organic part of the exposition of the text, to the degree that "the facts have affected the Habakkuk text."[2] Either the sect knew and used variant readings or made deliberate corrections to Habakkuk to achieve their purposes. Stendahl includes both possibilities but leans towards the latter, so that "in many cases DSH appears to be created *ad hoc* ."[3]

---

[1]*School* , 183–202. B. Gärtner, "The Habakkuk Commentary (DSH) and the Gospel of Matthew," *ST* 8 (1954), 1–24, offers a critique of this portion of Stendahl's argument. He denies that the Habakkuk scroll was produced by a *pesher* type of exegesis.
[2]*School* , 197.
[3]*School* , 189.

It is Stendahl's hypothesis that in the formula quotations the biblical text is treated in somewhat the same manner as in the DSH quotations. On the other hand, non-formula quotations are considered to be taken from the Greek text common to the church and synagogue.[1]

Robert Horton Gundry

Gundry's book, *The Use of the Old Testament in St. Matthew's Gospel with Special Reference to the Messianic Hope* ,[2] published in 1967, originated as a 1961 Ph.D. dissertation.

Gundry observes that the foundation of Stendahl's school hypothesis is the distinctiveness of the text-form of the formula quotations in Matthew, when compared to other Matthean OT quotations. In contrast to Stendahl, Gundry states that "the Matthaean formula-citations do not stand out from other synoptic quotation material in their divergence from the LXX, but the formal quotations in the Marcan (and parallel) tradition stand out in their adherence to the LXX."[3]

Following are some of Gundry's summary observations.[4] The formal quotations in Mark are almost slavishly Septuagintal, even where the LXX departs markedly from the Hebrew text. In the parallel quotations Matthew tends to depart slightly from both Mark and the LXX. The only formal quotations common to Matthew and Luke but absent in Mark occur in the temptation narrative. Two of these are Septuagintal; the other two likely are not. The formal quotations peculiar to Matthew, the formula quotations, are not homogeneous in text-form; they range from purely Septuagintal to wholly non-Septuagintal.

---

[1]Stendahl notes that "the striking thing about such an interpretation of Matthew's formula quotations is that we should have two types of quotation side by side in the same gospel, both the liturgical type and the *pesher* type" (*School* , 203). He resolves this difficulty by suggesting that there exists a different *Sitz im Leben* for each type of quotation (p. 205). The formula quotations are the "fruits of the creative activity of the Matthaean church."
[2]Leiden, E. J. Brill.
[3]*Use of the Old Testament* .
[4]These summary observations are found at the beginning of each group of quotations and in even greater detail at 147–150.

Gundry finds "two facts ... outstanding and indisputable": (1) the formal quotations in the Marcan tradition are almost purely Septuagintal; (2) all quotations in every other stratum of the synoptic material present a mixed textual tradition. The latter stands in contrast to the prevailingly Septuagintal form of OT quotations in the rest of the NT.

Gundry asserts that Stendahl is mistaken in believing that the mixed text-form formula quotations were the final stage in the development of the book of Matthew. Rather, the formula quotations might belong to the most primitive layer of tradition.

Gundry attacks Stendahl's position by undermining the monolithic character of the formula quotations. In general, Gundry notes that Stendahl failed to give serious consideration to non-Septuagintal quotations outside the formula quotations.

Gundry's attack on Stendahl becomes more specific in his following observations. First, the quotations peculiar to Matthew in the sermon on the mount, which are not preceded by fulfilment formulae, differ from the LXX as much as the formula quotations do. Second, those quotations which are located in the course of the double or triple tradition but are found only in Matthew are Septuagintal. If these come from the Matthean school, one would expect non Septuagintal form. If they are not from the Matthean school, why are the quotations peculiar to Matthew in the sermon on the mount not likewise Septuagintal?

Gundry proposes that the apostle Matthew was a note-taker during the earthly ministry of Jesus and that his notes provided the basis for most of the apostolic gospel tradition. Matthew the apostle stood apart from the other, unlettered apostles in his literacy. As a Levite he would have been familiar with the OT in its Semitic forms. As an ex-publican near Capernaum he would be fluent in Greek and have the habit of note-taking. "We can then understand how all strands of textual tradition made their way into the whole of the synoptic material, for the looseness and informality of such notes made it possible for Hebrew, Aramaic, and Greek all to appear in them." Gundry argues that there was only one place where Hebrew, Aramaic, and

Greek were all used in NT times: Palestine.[1] Hence, Palestine must have
been the origin of a document in which textual elements from all three
languages were so intimately intertwined, even within single quotations, as
to defy unravelling and preclude the supposition of redactional stages.

The notes of the apostle Matthew circulated in varying forms, from
which the three evangelists drew. Some forms of the notes may have been
expanded; sections of the notes may have circulated independently. This
would explain the fact that Matthew and Luke do not always agree exactly in
the Q material, and the difficulty in defining the boundaries of Q. It would
also explain why there is broad agreement among the synoptics concerning
the material included in the story of Jesus' life and ministry, when only a
fraction of what took place and was spoken has been selected. Otherwise,
the tradition would have been "hopelessly fragmented, and no synoptic
problem would exist." Such a single authoritative apostolic source would
also explain the persistent feeling that Mark is sometimes parallel to Q or
used Q.

When the mixed text of much of the synoptic tradition is held up
against the predominantly Septuagintal form of quotations in the rest of the
NT, and when it is noted that this mixed text occurs in all three synoptics,
Gundry finds a common body of tradition behind all three gospels.

George M. Soares Prabhu

Soares Prabhu's book, *The Formula Quotations in the Infancy
Narrative of Matthew: An Enquiry into the Tradition History of Mt 1–2* ,
originated in his 1969 doctoral dissertation.[2] He concluded that the formula

---

[1]Gundry goes into detail on "the hardcore archaeological evidence" which, for him, proves
that all three languages were commonly used by Jews in first-century Palestine. He
suggests that it is likely that Jesus himself and the apostles commonly spoke Greek in
addition to the Semitic languages. Hence, much of the gospel tradition would originally
have been cast into all three languages (*Use of the Old Testament* , 174–178).

[2]Soares Prabhu is to be credited both with admitting that the two-document hypothesis is
a presupposition of his work, and with realizing that it is "a convenient working
hypothesis" and not simply to be accepted as "a dogma of critical orthodoxy." He states
that he "would heartily endorse" the assertion of E. P. Sanders that "the difficulty with the
present situation is not that there is a dominant hypothesis, but that the dominant

quotations of Matthew are a unified group with a common origin and a common function, and that the formula quotations were inserted by the latest editor of the gospel, Matthew.

He begins by confronting the dual problem with which such an analysis must deal, that of the definition of "formula quotation" and the identification of the formula quotations.

Soares Prabhu defines or characterizes the formula quotations as possessing three features. The first of these is that they are introduced by a fulfilment formula unlike anything else found in the NT,[1] found only occasionally in the OT (1 Kgs 2:27; 2 Chr 36:21, 22; Ezra 1:1) and absent in post-biblical Jewish literature.[2] Matthew himself created the *Grundform* of these formulae, based on its OT analogues. He then modified this *Grundform* so that in every case it was adapted to its particular context of usage. Such an exact adaptation to the context of the finished gospel, Soares Prabhu reasons, can scarcely be the chance result of bringing together disparate sources, and provides evidence that this was at the redactional stage. All formulae are constructed around the verb πληροῦν and present an OT text as having been fulfilled by the event narrated.

The second characteristic of the formula quotation is that it serves a commentary function, in that it is an "aside" of the evangelist and not part of his narrative. On this basis these quotations have been called "Reflexionszitate," in contrast to the "Kontextzitate" which are part of the gospel narrative itself.[3] The term *Reflexionszitate* has been replaced by the more descriptive *Erfüllungszitate* and "formula quotations."[4]

---

hupothesis is frequently held too rigidly ... and is accorded a degree of certainty it does not merit" (*Formula Quotations* , 42, 43, n. 218).

[1]The subject of the formula itself is dealt with at 46–63.

[2]B. M. Metzger finds none in the Mishnah ("The Formulas Introducing Quotations of Scripture in the New Testament and the Mishnah," *JBL* 70 [1951], 307, n. 18).

J. Fitzmyer finds none in the Qumran material ("The Use of Explicit Old Testament Quotations in Qumran Literature and in the New Testament," *NTS* 7 [1960–1961], 330).

[3]Soares Prabhu notes that, except for Mark 1:2 and its parallels, the formula quotations are the only quotations in the synoptic gospels which are not part of the direct speech of Jesus or some other character in a narrative (*Formula Quotations* , 19).

[4]This term was used by S. E. Johnson ("The Biblical Quotations in Matthew," *HTR* 36 [1943], 135) although he did not indicate that he initiated its use.

The third characteristic of the formula quotations is that they have a mixed text form, different from the strongly Septuagintal form of Matthew's other citations. "The formula quotations of Mt have a text-type which agrees neither with the LXX, nor with the Masoretic Hebrew, nor with any version we know — though there are sporadic resemblances to the OT Peschitta, and even to one or other of the newer Greek versions."[1] In addition, the formula quotations do not present a uniform text-type. Their degree of agreement with or difference from the LXX and/or the MT differs from quotation to quotation. Soares Prabhu then provides profuse examples from Stendahl and Gundry,[2] but unlike Gundry, who sees some Septuagintal formula quotations (Matt 1:23; 3:3; 13:14–15), he asserts that "the formula quotations are ... by and large distinctly non-Septuagintal — though some are more non-Septuagintal than others."[3]

Soares Prabhu asserts that the LXX was not Matthew's Bible. He was unable to find even "one certain instance" where Matthew assimilated to the LXX any quotation borrowed from Mark.[4] In fact, he found two cases (Matt 19:4–5; 22:37) in which Matthew's version is less Septuagintal than Mark's. Three others (Matt 22:32; 26:31; 27:46) were ambiguous, with some elements more Septuagintal than in Mark, others less so. In only three cases (Matt 15:8–9; 19:18–19; 22:24) did he see even the possibility of assimilation to the LXX, "but even here, the contacts with the LXX are so slight (15:8–9), so indecisive (19:18–19), or so uncertain (22:24), that it would be rash to affirm positively that these are examples of a deliberate assimilation of non-Septuagintal (or rather, not fully Septuagintal) Markan quotations to the LXX." Based on this mixed evidence Soares Prabhu's conclusion is that any systematic redactional revision is ruled out. If there was any assimilation to the LXX, it took place at a pre-redactional stage, by means of standardization for the liturgical and catechetical use of the community. Such a pre-redactional adaptation would explain the confused textual condition of Matthew's synoptic context quotations.

---

[1] Soares Prabhu, *Formula Quotations* , 63.
[2] *Formula Quotations* , 63–64.
[3] *Formula Quotations* , 64.
[4] *Formula Quotations* , 83.

Soares Prabhu suggests that Matthew's *Vorlage* is the Hebrew text. He bases this on the freedom of the translation techniques of the time, as witnessed in the LXX and the Targum. At the same time Matthew would have used the LXX, the Bible of his church, to correct the Septuagintal quotations of his sources, and even to add new ones. The LXX/Hebrew dichotomy between the context and the formula quotations is not a rigid one. There are traces of Septuagintal language in the formula quotations, and the context quotations are not all from the LXX. Close adaptation of quotation to context excludes the possibility of random borrowing by Matthew and provides evidence of the Matthean origin of the quotation.

Soares Prabhu claims that the the formula quotations are not simply a convenient way of collecting "a heterogeneous collection of superfically similar quotations," but an objective group of quotations which have a common origin and a common function. It is the coincidence of the three distinctive features which puts this beyond doubt. "That just those quotations which are introduced by fulfilment formulas should be the ones that are comments of the evangelist, and have the same unusual text-type can scarcely be accidental!"[1] That the formula quotations are dispersed widely over the whole gospel, in material of varied origin (triple, double, and special traditions), indicates that these quotations belong to the final redactional stratum of the gospel, to Matthew himself.[2]

Having defined the formula quotations, then, as "a group of quotations with a common origin, and a common function, all belonging to the same tradition-historical stratum,"[3] Soares Prabhu next turns his attention to the identification of these quotations. Surveying the literature, he finds ten quotations which appear on every list: Matt 1:22–23; 2:15; 2:17–18; 2:23; 4:14–16; 8:17; 12:17–21; 13:35; 21:4–5; 27:9–10.[4] The status of four others (2:5–6; 13:14–15; 26:54; 26:56) appears open to discussion. These have some, but not all, of the three defining features of the formula quotations.

---

[1]*Formula Quotations* , 23.

[2]*Formula Quotations* , 41.

[3]*Formula Quotations* , 26.

[4] This seems a strange statement when only a few sentences before Soares Prabhu had remarked that most recent works set the group at ten or eleven quotations, but do not all agree on the same ten or eleven (24–25).

Hence, their appearance on, or absence from, a list of formula quotations will depend on which of these features has been chosen as the distinguishing mark of the group. One other quotation (3:3) is sometimes included because it is introduced by a formula resembling the fulfilment formulae, and it is a *Reflexionszitat*.. Finally, the quotation from Ps 22:19 is found at Matt 27:35 in some manuscripts, but appears on none of the lists because it is an obvious interpolation, possibly from John 19:24. Soares Prabhu affirms the usual ten quotations and adds only Matt 2:5–6 to his list of formula quotations. The latter, he believes, was originally a context quotation belonging to the pre-redactional Herod narrative. Later it was redactionally assimilated into the formula quotation group.

Summary

Holtzmann believed there were two major text-types in Matthew's OT quotations: (1) those from the LXX, and in common with Mark, (2) those reflecting the Hebrew text, and peculiar to Matthew. He suggested that these two text-types indicate that Matthew incorporated into his text those Septuagintal quotations he found in source A (preserved in our Mark), and added others based on the Hebrew text. For Holtzmann, then, the OT quotations in Matthew fall into a pattern of text-types that supports the two-document hypothesis.

While it was the purpose of neither Stendahl, nor Gundry, nor Soares Prabhu to demonstrate the relevance of the OT quotations in the synoptics to the study of the synoptic problem, their work is important for our study because they have attempted to determine the various text-types evident in the Matthean quotations.

Like Holtzmann, Stendahl finds that the quotations common to Matthew and Mark are of a fairly pure Septuagintal text-type, and that the formula quotations in Matthew are non-Septuagintal. However, against Holtzmann, he finds that the formula quotations of Matthew are of a mixed text-type, not simply based on the Hebrew. What is more significant for our purpose is that Stendahl finds some quotations peculiar to Matthew which are Septuagintal. This group militates against Holtzmann's overly simplistic use of the two text-types to affirm Marcan priority.

Contrary to Stendahl, Gundry claims that in Matthew all the formal quotations shared with Mark are purely Septuagintal. All other OT quotations in Matthew are of mixed text-types, and some of these are Septuagintal.

Soares Prabhu, like Stendahl, divides the Matthean OT quotations into two groups: (1) the formula quotations (which for Stendahl are of mixed text-type), (2) the remaining quotations (which for Stendahl are Septuagintal). Unlike Stendahl, Soares Prabhu sees all formula quotations as free translations of the Hebrew, rather than eclectic texts. As well, he considers some non-formula quotations non-Septuagintal. At the same time, like Stendahl, he grants that some formula quotations closely resemble the LXX. These perceptions badly blur the boundary between Holtzmann's two groups.

Soares Prabhu notes that scholars do not agree on what quotations comprise the group called "formula quotations." Their choice depends on which characteristic(s), of the three Soares Prabhu considers to define what a formula quotation is, they stress. It should come as no surprise, then, that there are at least three designations for this group of quotations: *Reflexionszitate* , *Erfüllungszitate* [1] (fulfilment quotations), formula quotations.

Indeed, there is so much debate over the characterization and selection of this group of quotations that G. Stanton asks whether the introductory formula is the *only* thing that distinguishes this group.[2] However, Ulrich Luz claims that fluidity in the form of the introductory formula allows for "gradations" from the formula quotations to "normal" quotations, so that distinctions between the former and the latter are "not unambiguous."[3] Luz asks why all the Matthean OT quotations did not

---

[1] Used at least since the time of Bleek, and still in use; cf. Wilhelm Rothfuchs, *Die Erfüllungszitate des Matthäus-Evangeliums* (Stuttgart: W. Kohlhammer, 1969).

[2] "The Origin and Purpose of Matthew's Gospel: Matthean Scholarship from 1945 to 1980," in Wolfgang Haase, ed., *Aufstieg und Niedergang der Römischen Welt* vol. 2; pt. 25; sect. 3 (Berlin: Walter de Gruyter, 1985) 1933.

[3] *Matthew 1–7: A Commentary* (Minneapolis: Augsburg, 1989) 156.

become formula quotations.[1] He suggests that in some cases the quotation did not refer directly to Jesus and so πληρόω was not a suitable introduction; in other cases Matthew knew that the quotation did not come from a prophetic book. When Matthew did use an introductory formula, it was to emphasize a theological theme.[2]

If, as Luz suggests, the use of an introductory formula has a lot to do with the content of the quotation, it should not be surprising that Gundry and Soares Prabhu find that the text-form of the formula quotations is sometimes similar to, or the same as, that of non-formula quotations.

Stendahl, Gundry, and Soares Prabhu all agree with Holtzmann that the OT quotations common to Mark and Matthew are Septuagintal. Holzmann's second claim, that all peculiarly Matthean quotations are based on the Hebrew, finds no support among the other three. Soares Prabhu comes closest when he says that the formula quotations are based on the Hebrew, but he also remarks that the non-formula, peculiarly Matthean quotations are Septuagintal, and even some of the formula quotations are almost Septuagintal. Gundry takes the latter claim one step further: some of the formula quotations *are* Septuagintal.

We can look at the peculiarly Matthean quotations in two ways. First, we can divide them into formula quotations and non-formula quotations. Stendahl, Gundry, and Soares Prabhu agree that some or all of the formula quotations are of a mixed text-type. Soares Prabhu says some are almost Septuagintal. Gundry asserts some are Septuagintal. Concerning the non-formula quotations, Stendahl and Soares Prabhu claim they are Septuagintal, while Gundry says they are of mixed text-types.

The second way of looking at the peculiarly Matthean quotations is to divide them into Septuagintal and non-Septuagintal. Concerning the Septuagintal quotations, Holtzmann is alone in finding none of these. Stendahl finds them only in non-formula quotations. Soares Prabhu finds them in non-formula quotations and almost in some formula quotations. Gundry finds them in formula and non-formula quotations.

---

[1]*Matthew 1–7* , 157.
[2]*Matthew 1–7* , 162.

What is immediately clear is that there is a decided difference of opinion among Stendahl, Gundry, and Soares Prabhu concerning the text-types of peculiarly Matthean OT quotations. Despite these differences, however, there is general agreement among the three that there are peculiarly Matthean Septuagintal quotations; the difference of opinion lies in their distribution. This point, if confirmed, would weaken, if not demolish, Holtzmann's argument. Because there exists such a range of opinion, and because the existence of peculiarly Matthean Septuagintal quotations militates against the good health of Holtzmann's case, the quotations need re-examination. Hence, we shall examine in detail the OT quotations in the synoptic gospels to see if the variety of text-types exhibited fall into a pattern which supports either the two-document hypothesis or the Griesbach position.

Chapter IV

Quotations Appearing in More than One Synoptic Gospel

In the ensuing discussion the quotations are presented in the following order. Quotations presented first are those which are found in more than one synoptic gospel, the text of which is identical or quite similar in those gospels. Those quotations which have similar or identical texts in three synoptics will be presented before those which are similar or identical in two synoptics. Quotations with an identical or similar text in two synoptics will precede those which occur in three synoptics but show greater diversity of text. This order of presentation cannot be exact; some might want to reverse the order of a few quotations here or there. Nevertheless, it has the merit of ranging the quotations over a gradient of similarity of text.

Where a citation appears in Matthew, this form of the citation will be given first. The text of a citation supplied in full, as it is found in the NT, will be the text found in the twenty-sixth edition of Nestle-Aland. The text of the LXX supplied in full will be that of the Göttingen edition. The text of the MT supplied in full will be from *Biblia Hebraica Stuttgartensia* . The texts of these major editions will often be referred to as "the preferred text." Manuscripts offering variant readings will be cited only where they are deemed to offer insight into resolution of our major problem.

With the exception of the following, symbols used for NT manuscript designation are identical to those found in the twenty-sixth edition of Nestle-Aland:[1]

M = Majority text

f^1 = minuscules of "family 1" (Lake group)

f^{13} = minuscules of "family 13" (Ferrar group).

Matthew 22:44

εἶπεν κύριος τῷ κυρίῳ μου· κάθου ἐκ δεξιῶν μου,

ἕως ἂν θῶ τοὺς ἐχθρούς σου ὑποκάτω τῶν ποδῶν σου

There are no significant variations for this text.

The preferred text of Mark 12:36 is identical to the preferred Matthean text. There is one significant variant: ὑποκάτω (B D W 28 sy[s] co)] υποποδιον (ℵ A L Θ Ψ 092b f[1] f[13] M lat sy[p.h]).

The editorial committee of the third edition of the United Bible Societies' *Greek New Testament*, the text of which is identical to that of the twenty-sixth edition of Nestle-Aland, gives ὑποκάτω a "C" rating. This rating indicates that "there is a considerable degree of doubt whether the text or the apparatus contains the superior reading."[2]

---

[1]Cf. Kurt Aland and Barbara Aland, *The Text of the New Testament: An Introduction to the Critical Editions and to the Theory and Practice of Modern Textual Criticism* (Grand Rapids: Eerdmans, 1987) 106–116.

Characteristics of particular manuscripts or groups of manuscripts which are stated in the textual discussions come principally from the following works: (1) for the NT: Aland and Aland, *Text of the New Testament* ; Bruce M. Metzger, *The Text of the New Testament: Its Transmission, Corruption, and Restoration* (2d ed.; Oxford: Clarendon, 1968); (2) for the LXX: the introductory sections of the various volumes of the Göttingen Septuagint; Sidney Jellicoe, *The Septuagint and Modern Study* (Oxford: Clarendon, 1968); (3) for other OT textual information: Bleddyn J. Roberts, *The Old Testament Text and Versions: The Hebrew Text in Transmission and the History of the Ancient Versions* (Cardiff: University of Wales Press, 1951); Ernst Würthwein, *The Text of the Old Testament: An Introduction to the Biblia Hebraica* ; tr. Erroll F. Rhodes from 4th ed. of *Der Text des Alten Testaments* (1973) (Grand Rapids: William B. Eerdmans, 1979). Where other sources of textual information are used they are cited as they occur.

[2]Bruce M. Metzger, *A Textual Commentary on the Greek New Testament* (London: United Bible Societies, 1975), xxviii.

Alexandrian manuscripts א and L, and the Caesarean Θ[1] witness
υποποδιον, while the Alexandrian B and the Western D witness ὑποκάτω.
Because D is particularly subject to parallel influence from the other gospels,[2] it does not influence a decision for the text. On this basis it is
impossible to decide in favor of either ὑποκάτω or υποποδιον.[3]

One argument for the original occurrence of ὑποκάτω in Mark is
particularly worth noting because it implies the hypothesis, which for our
purposes is in question, that Matthew used Mark. Bruce M. Metzger
considers "the priority of the Gospel according to Mark" to be one of the
criteria of gospel text criticism used to decide the text.[4] Because ὑποκάτω
occurs in the preferred text of the Matthean parallel, as opposed to
υποποδιον found in the LXX, Matthew must have found ὑποκάτω in
Mark. Copyists working later on the book of Mark would have altered the
original ὑποκάτω to υποποδιον because this is the "correct" reading found
in the Septuagint, witnessed in the parallel Luke 20:43 and in Acts 2:35.[5]

---

[1]Larry W. Hurtado, *Text-critical Methodology and the Pre-Caesarean Text: Codex W in
the Gospel of Mark* (Grand Rapids: Eerdmans, 1981) 87, 88, notes that Western
influence is seen so strongly in Θ that it should be regarded as the second best Greek
representative of the Western text of Mark, even though it does have Caesarean flavor.

[2]Krister Stendahl, *The School of St. Matthew and its Use of the Old Testament* (2nd ed.;
Lund: C. W. K. Gleerup, 1968), 78, n. 2.

[3]For various reasons different scholars have favored ὑποκάτω. M.-J. Lagrange does so on
the authority of B and D (*Évangile selon Saint Marc* (Paris: Gabalda, 1929) 326),
Stendahl, *The School* , 78, and Robert Horton Gundry, *The Use of the Old Testament in
St. Matthew's Gospel with Special Reference to the Messianic Hope* (Leiden: E. J. Brill,
1967) 25, claim that ὑποκάτω comes from the influence of Ps 8:7. Neither gives a full
argument for such a position. Both refer to other NT passages in which Ps 109:1 or Ps
8:7 are cited. Gundry states that "the quotations in Heb and 1 Cor illustrate the freedom
with which the similar expressions in Ps 110 [LXX Ps 109] and Ps 8 were interchanged."
However, when these are checked, where ἐχθρούς (Heb 1:13) or ἐχθροί (Heb 10:13)
appear, which indicate reference to Ps 109:1, so does ὑποπόδιον. Where there is no
reference to enemies, and the reference is obviously to Ps. 8:7, ὑποκάτω appears. The
writer of Hebrews seems, then, to have had no difficulty in keeping his references clear.
There is no reason why Mark would not have been equally clear.
    Cf. as well, A. E. J. Rawlinson who argues that Mark had ὑποκάτω on grounds
that he used Ps 8:6 as justification for the Son of Man title (*St Mark, with Introduction,
Commentary, and Additional Notes* (London: Methuen, 1925) 175). In a similar vein
Rudolf Pesch notes the combination of Ps 8:6 with 110:1 in 1 Cor 15:25–27; Eph 1:20–
22; Heb 1:3; 2:6–8 (*Das Marcusevangelium*, vol.2 (Freiburg: Herder, 1977) 254).

[4]Cited in both *Textual Commentary* , xxviii, and *Text of the New Testament* , 210.

[5]*Textual Commentary* , 111. Robert G. Bratcher and Eugene A. Nida argue that Mark
must have ὑποκάτω on the grounds that υποποδιον would be an assimilation to the
LXX (*A Translator's Handbook on the Gospel of Mark* (Leiden: Brill, 1961) 388).

Luke 20:42–43 has the same preferred text as Matthew except that ὑποπόδιον is in place of ὑποκατω.

The preferred LXX text (Ps 109:1) is identical to the Matthean text with the following exceptions: κύριος] ο κυριος; ὑποκάτω] υποποδιον. There are no significant variants.

The MT text (Ps 110:1) is:

נְאֻם יְהוָה לַאדֹנִי שֵׁב לִימִינִי
עַד־אָשִׁית אֹיְבֶיךָ הֲדֹם לְרַגְלֶיךָ

This agrees with the LXX virtually throughout. The LXX was in this case undoubtedly the text used by the evangelists.[1]

If both used Mark, as the two-document hypothesis suggests, why does Matthew have ὑποκάτω and Luke ὑποπόδιον? Gundry notes "the occasional assimilation to the LXX in Lk."[2] Holtzmann claimed that Luke would on occasion simply open the LXX and copy.[3] It could be argued that in this citation Luke has referred to the LXX.

If this were the case, and Mark had ὑποκάτω, an argument could be made for the two-document hypothesis. If ὑποπόδιον were the original Marcan text, the evidence of this citation would favor the Griesbach position. Here Matthew would have ὑποκάτω, Luke would use Matthew (and therefore use this Psalm citation in the same narrative context) but correct the citation to the LXX, and Mark, who refers to both Matthew and Luke, noting the difference in the citation, would check the LXX and go with Luke's version. Because the Marcan text is undecided, this quotation offers support for neither the two-document nor the Griesbach position over the other.

Charles Cutler Torrey sees ὑποκάτω slipping into Mark from Matthew by assimilation (*Documents of the Primitive Church* [New York: Harper & Brothers, 1941] 82).

[1] For an opposing view see W. F. Albright and C. S. Mann, *Matthew: Introduction, Translation, and Notes* (Garden City, New York: Doubleday, 1971) 275.

[2] *The Use of the Old Testament*, 184.

[3] *Die synoptischen Evangelien: Ihr Ursprung und geschichtlicher Charakter* (Leipzig: Engelmann, 1863) 263.

Matt 3:3

φωνὴ βοῶντος ἐν τῇ ἐρήμῳ·
ἑτοιμάσατε τὴν ὁδὸν κυρίου,
εὐθείας ποιεῖτε τάς τρίβους αὐτοῦ.

The parallel citation in Mark 1:3 has a text identical to that of the preferred Matthean text.

The preferred text of the citation in the parallel Luke 3:4 is also identical to the Matthean text as far as the latter goes. However, Luke continues on in vv. 5, 6 with the Isaiah text in fairly close agreement with the LXX:

πᾶσα φάραγξ πληρωθήσεται
καὶ πᾶν ὄρος καὶ βουνὸς ταπεινωθήσεται,
καὶ ἔσται τὰ σκολιὰ εἰς εὐθείαν
καὶ αἱ τραχεῖαι εἰς ὁδοὺς λείας·
καὶ ὄψεται πᾶσα σὰρξ τὸ σωτήριον τοῦ θεοῦ.

There is one significant variant reading: εὐθείαν (ℵ A C L W Θ Ψ f¹ f¹³ M it)] ευθειας (B D Ξ 892 pc lat; Or).

It is only with the twenty-sixth edition of Nestle-Aland that εὐθείαν replaced ευθειας in v. 5 as the preferred text. In favor of εὐθείαν is the majority of Alexandrian witnesses, including the proto-Alexandrian ℵ, the Majority text, the Caesarean (Θ f¹ f¹³), and most other manuscripts. In support of ευθειας, there is the proto-Alexandrian B and the Western D and the fact that, unlike εὐθείαν, this text could not have resulted from assimilation to the LXX. Hence, while the external evidence seems to favor εὐθείαν, the case is not a decisive one by any means.

The LXX for Isa 40:3 differs from the Matthean citation only in that instead of αὐτοῦ there is τοῦ θεοῦ ἡμῶν. The preferred text of the LXX for that part of Isa 40:4, 5 cited by Luke differs from the Lucan citation in the following respects: πάντα is inserted in the LXX after ἔσται; αἱ τραχεῖαι] ἡ τραχεῖα; the whole of Isa 40:5 in the LXX reads καὶ ὀφθήσε-

ται ἡ δόξα κυρίου, καὶ ὄψεται πᾶσα σάρξ τὸ σωτήριον τοῦ θεοῦ·
ὅτι κύριος ἐλάλησε of which Luke selected only καὶ ὄψεται πᾶσα σάρξ
τὸ σωτήριον τοῦ θεου.

Only one variant reading for that part of Isa 40:4, 5 cited by Luke
merits discussion here: παντα] omitted by A V and several minuscules,
marked with an obelus (indicating that this is not found in the Hebrew) by Q
and the Syro-Hexaplar.

Although A is a strong witness to the Alexandrian text, the omission
of παντα by A, V, and several minuscules is simply an assimilation to the
Hebrew, or even to Luke. Ziegler characterizes A as assimilating in several
places to the NT.[1] What argues for the retention of παντα in the original
text is that it is found in the strongest witness to the Alexandrian text, Q, but
marked with an obelus, indicating that the scribes of Q were aware that
παντα was not in the Hebrew. That they kept it indicates it was in their
exemplar.

The MT text for Isa 40:3 reads:

קוֹל קוֹרֵא
בַּמִּדְבָּר פַּנּוּ דֶּרֶךְ יְהוָה
יַשְּׁרוּ בָּעֲרָבָה מְסִלָּה לֵאלֹהֵינוּ

That part of Isa 40:4, 5 cited by Luke alone, in the MT reads:

כָּל־גֶּיא יִנָּשֵׂא וְכָל־הַר וְגִבְעָה יִשְׁפָּלוּ
וְהָיָה הֶעָקֹב לְמִישׁוֹר וְהָרְכָסִים לְבִקְעָה:
וְנִגְלָה כְּבוֹד יְהוָה וְרָאוּ כָל־בָּשָׂר יַחְדָּו

The preferred text of the LXX for the Matthean citation (Isa 40:3)
follows the MT closely in the first part (כָּל ... יְהוָה; φωνή ... κυρίου).
Both use the imperative for both verbs. However, the phrase בָּעֲרָבָה finds
no equivalent in the Greek, and the plural τὰς τρίβους does not accurately
render the singular מְסִלָּה. The gospel citation is, therefore, taken from the

---

[1] *Septuaginta* , vol.14: *Isaias*, 27. Ziegler does not cite this passage as one of his
examples.

LXX.[1] The αὐτοῦ replaces τοῦ θεοῦ ἡμῶν because the application is to Christ and not to Yahweh.[2]

A comparison of the citation of Isa 40:4, 5 as found in Luke with that in the LXX and the MT proves of value in determining what text Luke uses when on his own. First, his omission of καὶ ὀφθήσεται ἡ δόξα κυρίου as found in the LXX, makes sense considering the application to Christ. Luke omits ὅτι κύριος ἐλάλησε as superfluous for his purposes. For Isa 40:5, then, Luke appears to use the LXX with reasonable omissions.

Luke is similar to the Hebrew in that he uses the plural αἱ τραχεῖαι, corresponding to the plural הָרְכָסִים, rather than the singular ἡ τραχεῖα found in the LXX. He also omits πάντα. This might seem to indicate that Luke uses the standard LXX text, but alters it himself to conform to the Hebrew. However, if this were the case, why does Luke not make other changes as well? For example, why did he not make the change so many late minuscules made, ταπεινωθήσεται to ταπεινωθησονται? Why did he not make changes similar to those which the Hexapla made, especially to the obvious forms of πεδία which would correspond to the Hebrew לְבִקְעָה? Hence, he does not seem to have used the Hebrew as a corrective to the LXX.

The question remains, then, where did he get the change αἱ τραχεῖαι from ἡ τραχεῖα? Likely Luke made this change himself as a matter of style. He selected the plural to correspond to the plural predicate εἰς ὁδοὺς λείας and the plural τὰ σκολιὰ εἰς εὐθείας of the previous parallel clause.

In conclusion, Luke does not use the Hebrew to make his own translation. He is too close to the LXX (πληρόω instead of ἐπαιρω for יִשָּׂא, for example) in everything but the omission of πάντα and his own stylistic change to αἱ τραχεῖαι from ἡ τραχεῖα to have used any other source. Even the omission of πάντα could have been for style, to give an exact parallelism between the two clauses, τὰ σκολιὰ εἰς εὐθείας and αἱ

---

[1]Cf. Gundry, *The Use of the Old Testament* , 9-10.
[2]So Stendahl, *The School* , 48, but not so Gundry, *The Use of the Old Testament* , 10.

τραχεῖαι εἰς ὁδοὺς λείας. What is of significance, and what has made this lengthy discussion worthwhile, is that in places where, on first glance, Luke may have appeared to have altered the LXX to the Hebrew, it is possible that he has simply made stylistic changes that coincidentally corresponded to places where the Hebrew differed from the LXX. A second possibility is that Luke's Isaiah text showed this much assimilation to the Hebrew, but we have no evidence for this.

Since the citation of Isa 40:3 is in an identical form for all three gospels,[1] and yet differs from the form found in the LXX in that τοῦ θεοῦ ἡμῶν is replaced by αὐτοῦ, little can be said except that the LXX was used but with an adaptation for Christian purposes. To be able to say anything about the synoptic relationship, we must go outside the citation itself.

Against Matthew and Luke, Mark has the Isaiah quotation preceded by a quotation from Exodus and/or Malachi found also in Matt 11:10 and Luke 7:27.[2] The idea connecting the citations in Mark is that of preparing τὴν ὁδόν (although two different Greek[3] verbs for "prepare" are used by Mark).

The problem for the Griesbach position here is why Mark omits the narrative common to Matthew (11:7–19) and Luke (7:24–35), but inserts its quotation at 1:2.

Under the two-document hypothesis the narrative common to Matthew and Luke but missing in Mark must be assigned to source Q. Coincidentally, Mark used at the beginning of his gospel (1:2) a quotation from Exodus/Malachi found also in Q (cf. Matt 11:10; Luke 7:27). Matthew and Luke, working independently of each other, would have chosen to omit

---

[1] Torrey (*Documents* , 45, 55) asserts that identical quotations are the result of the evangelists' striving to present a "solid front." He claims it was felt to be desirable that quotations found in two or more of the Greek gospels should agree with one another as well as with the LXX.

[2] W. D. Davies and Dale C. Allison make a few suggestions: (1) that Matthew and Luke took this quotation from Mark but omitted Mark 1:2 because it was not from Isaiah as the introductory formula states (*A Critical and Exegetical Commentary on the Gospel According to Saint Matthew* , vol.1 [Edinburgh: T. & T. Clark, 1988] 292–294); (2) that Q had one quotation here and another at the Matt 11 location ("in the wilderness" here in both Matthew and Luke suggests Q).

[3] The conjuction of פנה and דרך are found in the MT of Mal 3:1 and Isa 40:3. This suggests that those familiar with the Hebrew may have originally grouped the two verses.

the Exodus/Malachi quotation in the context of Matt 3:3 and Luke 3:4, perhaps because they realized it could not follow an introductory formula naming Isaiah as the source for the quoted material. That the quotation was to be cited later in their gospels may also have been a factor in the omission.[1] The coincidental omission of Mark 1:2 in Matthew and Luke is problematic, but perhaps easier explained than the procedure required by the Griesbach hypothesis. Thus the evidence for this quotation seems slightly to favor the two-document hypothesis.

Matt 21:42

λίθον ὃν ἀπεδοκίμασαν οἱ οἰκοδομοῦντες,
οὗτος ἐγενήθη εἰς κεφαλὴν γωνίας·
παρὰ κυρίου ἐγένετο αὕτη
καὶ ἔστιν θαυμαστὴ ἐν ὀφθαλμοῖς ἡμῶν;

There are no significant variants from the preferred text of the twenty-sixth edition of Nestle-Aland.

The preferred text of this citation in the parallel Mark 12:10–11 is identical to that in Matthew. There are no variant manuscripts listed in Nestle-Aland for the Marcan text.

The preferred text of this citation in the parallel Luke 20:17 is identical to that of the first two lines in Matthew and Mark (λίθον ὃν ἀπεδοκίμασαν οἱ οἰκοδομοῦντες, οὗτος ἐγενήθη εἰς κεφαλὴν γωνίας·), but omits the last two lines (παρὰ κυρίου ἐγένετο αὕτη καὶ ἔστιν θαυμαστὴ ἐν ὀφθαλμοῖς ἡμῶν).[2] There are no variant manuscripts listed in Nestle-Aland for the Lucan text.

The preferred text of the LXX (Ps 117:22–23) is identical to that of Matthew and Mark. Variants in the LXX text as cited by Rahlfs are few and insignificant.

The MT text (Ps 118:22–23) is:

---

[1]*Die synoptischen Evangelien* , 261–262.
[2]See Traugott Holtz, *Untersuchungen über die alttestamentlichen Zitate bei Lukas* (Berlin: Academic Press, 1968) 161, for an explanation of Luke's omission.

אֶבֶן מָאֲסוּ הַבּוֹנִים הָיְתָה לְרֹאשׁ פִּנָּה
מֵאֵת יְהוָה הָיְתָה זֹּאת הִיא נִפְלָאת בְּעֵינֵינוּ

The LXX and the MT correspond closely for this passage, except
for the καί before the last clause of the Greek. The exact wording, including
the καί, of the LXX is found in all three gospels, indicating that the LXX
was the source of this citation.

Matthew could have used Mark here, or Mark could have used
Matthew. Because the form of quotation is identical in both books, there are
no grounds for choosing either the Griesbach or two-document position
over the other. The fact that Luke lacks Ps 117:23 (LXX) does not help a
decision. In Griesbach terms, Mark would have chosen Matthew's longer
version over Luke's abbreviated quotation. On the basis of the two-
document hypothesis, Matthew does not know Luke. In a discussion of this
quotation, Luke is not a necessary source in either viewpoint. The only
question would be why Luke abbreviated the quotation he found in his
source (Mark or Matthew), and this does not bear on our problem.

Matt 15:4b

ὁ κακολογῶν πατέρα ἢ μητέρα θανάτῳ τελευτάτω.

There are no textual variations in Nestle-Aland for this citation.

The parallel preferred text of Mark 7:10b is identical to that of
Matthew. The Marcan text has no significant variants.

The LXX for Exod 21:16 has the same text as the Matthean citation.
The MT text for Exod 21:17 reads:

וּמְקַלֵּל אָבִיו וְאִמּוֹ מוֹת יוּמָת:

The LXX shows some variance to the Hebrew. The usual LXX
rendering for קלל is καταρᾶσθαι rather than the κακολογεῖν employed
here.

The gospel form of the citation comes from the LXX, rather than the Hebrew. It uses κακολογεῖν which does not correspond to the Hebrew קלל.

Because the Matthean and Marcan citations are identical, and there is nothing in the citation which indicates it would fit more neatly into either the Matthean or Marcan context, it is impossible to derive any conclusions regarding the synoptic relationship here. Nevertheless, some useful observations can be made.

Since the wording in the context of the quotation is so different in the two gospels, it is remarkable that the wording of the citation itself is identical. This suggests that Matthew used Mark, Mark used Matthew, or they both used the LXX. In other words, unless we are to attribute the identical quotation in the gospels to scribal assimilation that has been so early and complete that no manuscript evidence remains to show this has happened, this citation offers very cogent evidence that some synoptic relationship does exist.

Matt 19:4[1]

---

[1]It is debatable whether this passage should be included in our discussion of the citations. It is not always a clear case whether a passage is a citation or simply an allusion. John C. Hawkins, in his discussion of quotations from the OT (*Horae Synopticae: Contributions to the Study of the Synoptic Problem* [Oxford: Clarendon, 1909] 154–156), does not include this passage in his list of quotations, nor does he include it with "other places in which Matthew, without expressly quoting ... seems to be influenced by ... [OT] language" (158).

On the other hand, Henry Barclay Swete does include it in his list of quotations from the LXX in the synoptic gospels (*An Introduction to the Old Testament in Greek* [1902; repr. New York: KTAV, 1968] 386–387). Swete's criterion for differentiating "formal" or "direct citations" from "mere allusions and reminiscences" is the presence of an introductory formula, or, in the absence of such, evidence that it was the intention of the NT writer to make a formal citation (381–382).

Intention of the writer must be determined, of course, by examination of the text. Swete suggests that either the context of the problematic passage, or the verbatim agreement of the NT passage with some OT passage, will indicate this intention of the writer or its lack. Stendahl simply adopts Swete's criteria (*The School* , 46). Judgment as to whether a passage is a formal citation or an allusion, then, must necessarily be subjective, and, hence, moot.

In Matt 19:4 Jesus asks the Pharisees if they have not read (ἀνέγνωτε), presumably in the scriptures, what follows. The previous verse indicates the general context is a discussion of the law, for which recourse must be to the content of the Torah. This suggests that citations from the Torah might be expected. Clearly v. 5 is meant to be a formal citation of the OT. Hawkins (*Horae Synopticae* , 155) does include this verse in his list of quotations, despite his exclusion of v. 4. While he gives no reason for

ἄρσεν καὶ θῆλυ ἐποίησεν αὐτούς

The preferred text of the parallel, Mark 10:6, is identical to the preferred text of Matthew. It is followed immediately by another OT citation, whereas in Matthew the two citations are separated by καὶ εἶπεν, which refers back to the speaker, Jesus. However, there is no attempt in Matthew to combine the two citations into one, or even to give the appearance that one citation is being offered.

The preferred text of the LXX for that part of Gen 1:27 cited in Matthew and Mark is identical to the latter. The full text for the verse reads:

καὶ ἐποίησεν ὁ θεὸς τὸν ἄνθρωπον, κατ᾽ εἰκόνα θεοῦ
ἐποίησεν αὐτόν, ἄρσεν καὶ θῆλυ ἐποίησεν αὐτούς.

The MT text for that part of Gen 1:27 which is cited in Matthew and Mark reads:

זָכָר וּנְקֵבָה בָּרָא אֹתָם׃

Since the LXX and the MT texts agree, the evangelists could have used either but, in view of the verbatim agreement with the LXX we must assume the LXX. Because the preferred texts of Matthew and Mark are identical, this citation itself offers an example which can provide no evidence vis-à-vis the synoptic problem.

The only hint of direction of usage lies outside the citation itself. It is possible that, realizing the verb ἐποίησεν had only an implicit subject in Mark, Matthew added ὁ κτίσας ἀπ᾽ ἀρχῆς to provide an explicit subject.

---

excluding v. 4, one is not difficult to find. The wording of the verse seems to suggest an indirect quote. While ὅτι can be used to introduce a direct quote, it can also indicate merely indirect quotation. Context will determine which. Here the text in question is preceded by οὐκ ἀνέγνωτε ὅτι ὁ κτίσας ἀπ᾽ ἀρχῆς, none of which appears in the OT text, suggesting that the ὅτι does not introduce a direct citation. Nothing in the context of the parallel passage, Mark 10:6, suggests direct citation either.

Nevertheless, two factors sway the decision in the other direction. One is the general context which leads the reader to expect direct quotation, and the direct citation in the following verse. The other factor is the word αὐτούς in the text in question. This has its place in the OT passage, but what does it refer back to here?

It is worth noting that he did not use ὁ θεός from the LXX. It is difficult to imagine Mark's changing Matthew's explicit subject to an implicit one. In this case the two-document position is favored over the Griesbachian.

A second possible alteration by Matthew of the Marcan text, also outside the citation itself, is the replacement of δέ with οὐκ ἀνέγνωτε. There are no textual variants for this in Matthew or Mark, and it is difficult to imagine why, if Matthew were used by Mark, Mark would have deleted the οὐκ ἀνέγνωτε. On the other hand, one can easily imagine Matthew adding this to Mark to draw attention to the fact that the following citation is a citation from the Torah, and, hence, makes it a valid reply by Jesus to the Pharisees.

Matt 22:39

> ἀγαπήσεις τὸν πλησίον σου ὡς σεαυτόν.

There are no variants listed in Nestle-Aland for this text.

The parallel preferred text in Mark 12:31 is identical to the Matthean version.

The preferred text of the citation in Luke 10:27b is identical to the Matthean and Marcan versions, provided the ἀγαπήσεις from the beginning of the verse in the previous citation is understood to be repeated immediately before τὸν πλησίον. Nestle-Aland lists no textual variants here. The principal difference is that in Matthew and Mark this citation is spoken by Jesus, whereas in Luke it is not.

This citation is identical to part of Lev 19:18 in the LXX.

The citation as it appears in the gospels is taken from the middle of Lev 19:18; in the MT this reads:

> וְאָהַבְתָּ לְרֵעֲךָ כָּמוֹךָ

Because the gospel citation is identical with the LXX, even in the use of the future ἀγαπήσεις, it has come from the LXX.

The Lucan quotation is placed in a different setting than that of Matthew and Mark. Here the discussion concerns eternal life and a lawyer utters the quotation; in Matthew and Mark the discussion concerns the commandments and the quotation appears on Jesus' lips. However, in both the two-document and Griesbach hypotheses Luke is not the primary source; either Matthew or Mark is. Because these two have identical wording in the citation, and there is no adaptation of context to citation in either case, it is impossible to draw any conclusions on which came first.

Matt 21:13

ὁ οἶκός μου οἶκος προσευχῆς κληθήσεται[1]

There are no textual variants listed in Nestle-Aland for this passage.

The Marcan parallel (Mark 11:17) is identical in its preferred text to the Matthean citation, but adds πᾶσιν τοῖς ἔθνεσιν.

The preferred text (found in Nestle-Aland) of the parallel in Luke 19:46 differs from the Matthean text in that ἔσται is added to the beginning and κληθήσεται is missing.

The preferred text of Isa 56:7 in the LXX differs from the Marcan text in two places: it inserts γάρ, beginning ὁ γὰρ οἶκος; it has πᾶσι where Mark has πᾶσιν. The latter is simply an orthographic difference. The γάρ is a conjunction joining the clause following to what goes before. Since Mark is not citing the whole verse, it makes sense to omit the γάρ.

The MT for Isa 56:7 reads:

כִּי בֵיתִי בֵּית־תְּפִלָּה יִקָּרֵא לְכָל־הָעַמִּים

The LXX and MT texts correspond closely. Verbatim agreement with the LXX indicates that it is the source for the quotation in the gospels.

---

[1]The verse continues with ὑμεῖς δὲ αὐτὸν ποιεῖτε σπήλαιον λῃστῶν. The words σπήλαιον λῃστῶν are an allusion to Jer 7:11.

Speculation on the synoptic dimension of this citation appears to lead nowhere. Assuming Marcan priority, Gundry[1] has suggested that Matthew omits πᾶσιν τοῖς ἔθνεσιν to avoid diverting Jewish readers from the main point, which supposedly is that the temple is a place for prayer, not business. Alternatively, if Matthew and Luke are both post-70 (as nearly all agree), there was no longer any point in calling the temple a place of worship for all nations, and coincidental omission of the Marcan phrase is not impossible. But this is far from certain.[2] If we assume the Griesbach hypothesis, Luke would have largely reproduced the quotation as he found it in Matthew; Mark, on the other hand, would have added πᾶσιν τοῖς ἔθνεσιν, perhaps for theological reasons, to show a mission to the gentiles. This might seem a simpler explanation than the coincident omission of a phrase in Mark by Matthew and Luke, as required by the two-document hypothesis. But the theological explanation for Mark's procedure is not entirely satisfactory either. If Mark wrote after Matthew and Luke he would surely know of the temple's destruction, and there was little to be gained by labelling the temple a location for the worship of all nations at such a time. Incidentally, Matthew's omission of πᾶσιν τοῖς ἔθνεσιν requires explanation on either hypothesis, either as an omission from Mark (the two-document hypothesis) or as one from Isaiah (the Griesbach position).

In any case, the use of theological arguments or arguments which presuppose the solution of introductory problems like audience and purpose of writing are not the best criteria for solving the synoptic problem.

Finally, Luke's use of ἔσται instead of the Hebraism κληθήσεται cannot tell us whether he used Mark or Matthew, or even rule out that he himself was the prior gospel, because Matthew and Mark could always have simply reverted to the LXX. This quotation is at least an example of the Septuagintal character of a quotation common to all three gospels, as Holtzmann's argument suggests.

---

[1] *The Use of the Old Testament* , 19.
[2] Nevertheless, Stendahl remarks, "Mark's πᾶσιν τοῖς ἔθνεσιν most clearly shows that this gospel's quotation is primary and that Matthew left it out as less important in the context" (*The School* , 67).

Matt 4:4

οὐκ ἐπ' ἄρτῳ μόνῳ ζήσεται ὁ ἄνθρωπος, ἀλλ' ἐπὶ παντὶ
ῥήματι ἐκπορευομένῳ διὰ στόματος θεοῦ.

The preferred text (א B L W 1241 *pc* sy^s sa bo^{pt}) of the parallel
citation in Luke 4:4 is identical to that of Matthew except that ἀλλ' ... θεοῦ
is lacking. There is a significant variant: αλλ ἐπι παντι ῥηματι θεου is
added by A (D) Θ Ψ (0102) f^{1}f^{13} *M* latt sy$^{p.h}$ bo^{pt}. In Matthew and Luke
codex Θ is among the Byzantine group, so that it and codex A only confirm
the Koine and offer no additional witness. Codex D is always suspect of
assimilation to the other synoptics. Nestle-Aland suggests assimilation to
the Matthean text here, as does Metzger.[1] This is likely the case. If the
longer form had been original with Luke, it would be necessary to explain
why so great a variety of text-types (including manuscripts like א and B)
have chosen to omit this latter clause. Hence, the preferred shorter text
stands.

The preferred text of the LXX for Deut 8:3 is identical to that of
Matthew except that it repeats ζήσεται ὁ ἄνθρωπος at the end, and uses
the article τῷ with ἐκπορευομένῳ.

The MT text for Deut 8:3 for the part cited in Matthew reads:

לֹא עַל־הַלֶּחֶם לְבַדּוֹ יִחְיֶה הָאָדָם כִּי עַל־כָּל־מוֹצָא פִּ־יְהֹוָה

It repeats יִחְיֶה הָאָדָם at the end, corresponding to the repetition at the end
of the LXX verse.

The LXX and MT correspond fairly closely except that the Hebrew
כָּל is expanded upon to yield the Greek παντὶ ῥήματι, יְהֹוָה is rendered
by θεοῦ, and διά is added. It is clear that the evangelists used the LXX
version.[2]

---

[1]*A Textual Commentary* , 137. Metzger also suggests assimilation to the LXX.
[2]Torrey (*Documents* , 55) counters that the fact that Matthew closely resembles the LXX
need not necessarily indicate dependence. Translation from the Hebrew is possible because
"there is no point at which the translation could naturally be altered." This is an argument
Torrey uses again and again.

If we assume the Griesbach position, Luke would have omitted the last half of the citation as it appears in Matthew. On the other hand, if this is Q material, in the two-document hypothesis, the shorter version would be in Q,[1] and Matthew would have filled it out with the LXX, the clause ἐκπορευομένῳ διὰ στόματος showing how accurately he followed the LXX. It is worth noting that here is a case of a non-Marcan quotation with Septuagintal form.

Matt 4:6

τοῖς ἀγγέλοις αὐτοῦ ἐντελεῖται περὶ σοῦ

... ἐπὶ χειρῶν ἀροῦσίν σε,

μήποτε προσκόψῃς πρὸς λίθον τὸν πόδα σου.

The preferred Lucan text (Luke 4:10–11) is identical to the preferred Matthean text except that τοῦ διαφυλάξαι σε is found after περί σου at the end of v. 11.

The preferred text of the LXX for Ps 90:11–12 is identical to the citation in Luke except that after τοῦ διαφυλάξαι σε is found ἐν πάσαις ταῖς ὁδοῖς σου.

The MT for Ps 91:11–12 reads:

G. D. Kilpatrick ("Mt iv.4," *JTS* 45 [1944], 176) claims that Matthew lacked ἐκπορευομένῳ διὰ στόματος. He states this claim on the basis of the text in codex D. Codex D usually has the fuller text and also tends to fill out a text according to the LXX. Since in this case it has the shorter text, it must, considering its characteristic fullness, preserve the original Matthean text.

A comment regarding the characteristics of D undermines this claim. While D often does have a fuller text, it also characteristically can have a shorter text (see, for example, Metzger, *The Text History of the New Testament* , 50). Hence, here it may simply be manifesting this characteristic. What is noteworthy about D is that it so often differs from the majority of other witnesses.

Gundry (*The Use of the Old Testament* , 67) also opts for a shorter Matthean text lacking ἐκπορευομένῳ διὰ στόματος.

[1]That Luke has Q, see Davies and Allison, *Matthew* , 363; that Matthew has Q, see H. Mahnke, *Die Versuchungsgeschichte im Rahmen der synoptischen Evangelien* (Bern: Lang, 1978) 60–61, and H. Schürmann, *Das Lukasevangelium* (Freiburg: Herder, 1969) 210, n.14.

כִּי מַלְאָכָיו יְצַוֶּה־לָּךְ לִשְׁמָרְךָ בְּכָל־דְּרָכֶיךָ
עַל־כַּפַּיִם יִשָּׂאוּנְךָ פֶּן־תִּגֹּף בָּאֶבֶן רַגְלֶךָ

The LXX renders the Hebrew closely. The gospels used the LXX, as common wording is extensive.

This citation provides a good example of a case where the LXX is cited accurately but part of it is left out as unnecessary for the narrative context. Here the devil challenges Jesus to leap from the pinnacle of the temple. The second verse cited, ἐπὶ χειρῶν ... τὸν πόδα σου, specifically covers protection from an incident such as that specified in the challenge. Therefore, it is only necessary to cite that part of the OT which mentions God commanding his angels to offer protection. It is unnecessary to include the elaboration of this protection for all cases (ἐν πάσαις ταῖς ὁδοῖς σου), when the narrative is dealing with only one case, and that one covered in the detail of the second verse cited.

Whoever (source Q, Matthew, Luke, etc.) in NT times was the first to use this citation, if we assume he wished to omit whatever was not necessary in the context of the narrative, could do two things. He could omit only ἐν πάσαις ταῖς ὁδοῖς σου, leaving the infinitive phrase τοῦ διαφυλάξαι σε as the natural continuation of the verb ἐντελεῖται, or he could also omit τοῦ διαφυλάξαι σε understanding ἐντελεῖται περὶ σοῦ in the sense of "give orders concerning you" or, as the RSV translates, "he will give his angels charge of you," so that τοῦ διαφυλάξαι σε is simply in apposition to ἐντελεῖται περὶ σοῦ. We see each of these options in Matthew and Luke. The problem is which option appeared first.

It would appear to make little sense to remove the infinitive phrase τοῦ διαφυλάξαι σε, if this were the form in which the NT tradition first appeared. Therefore, either Matthew was used by Luke, as Griesbach would have it, or Matthew's version appeared in Q, as the two-document hypothesis would have it. The longer version in Luke is a result of Luke's understanding the need for an infinitive to complete ἐντελεῖται. Observations regarding this citation, then, favor neither the Griesbach hypothesis nor the two-document hypothesis over the other.

Matt 4:7

οὐκ ἐκπειράσεις κύριον τὸν θεόν σου.

The parallel text in Luke 4:12 is identical to its Matthean counterpart.
For Deut 6:16 the LXX has a text identical to that cited in Matthew.
In the MT Deut 6:16 reads:

לֹא תְנַסּוּ אֶת־יְהוָה אֱלֹהֵיכֶם

Unlike the Hebrew, which uses the second plural in the cited
passage, the LXX uses the second singular. In the LXX this is a consistent
difference throughout the chapter, and probably is a result of understanding
the people of Israel as a single entity, whereas here the Hebrew speaks to
the people as many people. The gospels have used the LXX.

Because the texts of Matthew and Luke are identical, nothing can be
said regarding their synoptic relationship. Note, however, the Septuagintal
form of this non-Marcan quotation.

Matt 4:10

κύριον τὸν θεόν σου προσκυνήσεις καὶ αὐτῷ μόνῳ
λατρεύσεις.

There are no variants listed in Nestle-Aland for this text.
The preferred text of the parallel Luke 4:8 is identical to the Matthean
text. There is one variant text cited in Nestle-Aland: κύριον τὸν θεόν σου
προσκυνήσεις (ℵ B D L W Ξ Ψ f¹ f¹³ 33 892 1241 1424 *al* lat syᵖ·ʰ)]
προσκυνησεις κυριον τον θεον σου (A Θ 0102 *M* a r¹).

Since the variant reading was the preferred text of the twenty-fifth
edition of Nestle-Aland, we should expect evidence for each reading to be
nearly equal. Strangely, this is not the case. In support of the variant

reading are A and Θ, both Koine in Luke.[1] For the preferred reading, א and B are proto-Alexandrian, among the very strongest witnesses to the original text, W is later Alexandrian for this part of Luke, f^1 and f^{13} are early Caesarean, and D is Western. Hence, there is a great geographical spread among witnesses to the preferred text. Why was the variant the favored text for so long? One can only guess. Probably it was due to the consideration of such possible internal evidence as that κύριον τὸν θεόν σου προσκυνήσεις could be simply an assimilation to the Matthean text. The preferred text stands.

For the cited text as found in Deut 6:13, the LXX has two variations from the Matthean citation: προσκυνήσεις] φοβηθήσῃ; μόνῳ] omitted.

The LXX text has only two variations of significance: φοβηθήσῃ] προσκυνησεις (A); the addition of μονω after αὐτῷ (A F V 963 and several whole families of manuscripts).

Because these are the very same variations that are in the text of the gospels there is the problem of whether the gospels used a text with the variations, such as one akin to A, or A was assimilated to the gospels.[2]

Since προσκυνήσεις is found only in A, the possibility of assimilation to the gospel text must certainly be explored. There are several strong points on the side of assimilation: (1) προσκυνήσεις is not used to translate ירא anywhere else in the LXX; (2) Codex A has used προσκυνησεις in place of φοβηθήσῃ, and added μονῳ after αὐτῷ in Deut 10:20, as well, again against the rest of the LXX tradition; (3) προσκυνήσεις is found in the preceding verse in both Matthew and Luke. This suggests that a change was made in the citation to correspond to this part of the narrative context, and that A's readings in Deuteronomy were assimilated to this.

The fact that papyrus 963 supports Codex A for the addition of μονῳ but not for the use of προσκυνησεις should not suggest that the former variation constituted the original text. Rather, this likely points to gradual assimilation to the gospel text. The witness of papyrus 963 really

---

[1]Metzger, The Text of the New Testament , 47, 58.
[2]For bibliographic details, see Gundry, The Use of the Old Testament , 68–69.

may only indicate that such assimilation started in the second century.[1] It is clear from this review of the evidence that the LXX preferred text stands. For that part of the text in the citation, the MT for Deut 6:13 reads:

אֶת־יְהוָה אֱלֹהֶיךָ תִּירָא וְאֹתוֹ תַעֲבֹד

The LXX corresponds exactly to the MT. The verbs are in the singular in both cases and the order of the wording is identical.

Here is a case where the gospels or the gospel tradition has used a text differing from both the LXX and the MT,[2] the latter two corresponding exactly. There certainly is no attempt to approach the MT.

If Codex A was assimilated to the gospel tradition, the question remains as to whence came προσκυνήσεις and μονω. The fact that προσ-κυνήσεις is found in the preceding verse in both Matthew and Luke suggests that the change was made in the citation to correspond to this part of the narrative context. The devil has just offered Jesus all the kingdoms of the world if Jesus will only worship (προσκυνήσεις) him. Jesus then answers by soundly rebuffing the devil with this OT citation. As well, the context would make the addition of μονω quite natural. Jesus is stressing that one should have "only" one master, God, not the devil nor God and the devil.

Both gospels have the identical text. Both have adapted the LXX text in the same way to the narrative setting. The narrative and its neatly fitting citation may, of course, have been in a tradition used by both, such as Q.

Matt 11:10

> ἰδοὺ ἐγὼ ἀποστέλλω τὸν ἄγγελόν μου πρὸ προσώπου σου,
> ὃς κατασκευάσει τὴν ὁδόν σου ἔμπροσθέν σου.

---

[1]So Gundry, *The Use of the Old Testament* , 69.
[2]Torrey (*Documents* , 56–57) here speculates on the wording of an earlier Hebrew version of Matthew he believes existed.

There are no variant texts listed in Nestle-Aland.

We shall examine the Lucan parallel next, because the Marcan citation is found in a different context. The preferred text of Luke 7:27 differs from the Matthean text only in that ἐγώ is lacking.

The citation as it appears in Mark 1:2 differs from the Matthean text in that it lacks ἐγώ and ἔμπροσθέν σου. There is a significant variant text: ιδου αποστελλω (B D Θ 28* 565 pc lat co; Ir^lat)] ιδου εγω αποστελλω (ℵ A L W f¹ f¹³ M vg^cl sy^h sa^ms bo^ms; Or Eus).

For the first variant text the external evidence is almost evenly balanced; for the inclusion of εγω there is a proto-Alexandrian witness in ℵ, a Western witness in W (for this part of Mark), and Koine witnesses; against, there is the proto-Alexandrian B, the Western D, and the Caesarean Θ. Perhaps the Caesarean witness might be considered to have slightly more weight than the Koine witnesses, but this is not enough to tip the balance. NT assimilation could go either way, to εγω as assimilation to Matthew, or excluding εγω as assimilation to Luke. The argument for assimilation is stronger in the direction of the LXX, which in Exod 23:20 includes ἐγώ. Hence, we may lean toward the exclusion of εγω, but the decision is not a clear one.

The first part of the Matthean citation, ἰδού ... προσώπου σου, corresponds exactly to Exod 23:20 as found in the LXX.

That portion of Exod 23:20 which is found in the Matthean citation, in the MT reads:

הִנֵּה אָנֹכִי שֹׁלֵחַ מַלְאָךְ לְפָנֶיךָ

The LXX corresponds to the MT particularly in rendering הִנֵּה with ἰδού, אָנֹכִי with ἐγώ, and לְפָנֶיךָ with πρὸ προσώπου σου, in quite literal fashion. For example, the only reason the Hebrew has אָנֹכִי is that this is grammatically necessary with the participle שֹׁלֵחַ; there is no reason for it to be translated in the Greek.

All three gospels retain the pronoun μου in contrast to the MT, which indicates that the gospel tradition used the LXX here. Also suggesting use of the LXX is the occurrence of ἀποστέλλω rather than the participle, which might result from a direct translation of the Hebrew. As well, the gospels have followed the literal translation of לְפָנֶיךָ by πρό προσώπου σου.

Matthew follows the LXX verbatim, as he includes ἐγώ, whereas Mark (if the preferred Marcan text is correct) and Luke do not.

The remainder of the citation as found in Matthew, ὅς κατασκευάσει τὴν ὁδόν σου ἔμπροσθέν σου, is often considered to come from Mal 3:1.[1] However, even a hasty glance at the LXX text of this passage proves that the dependence is at least not Septuagintal. It reads:

ἰδοὺ ἐγὼ ἐξαποστέλλω τὸν ἄγγελόν μου,
καὶ ἐπιβλέψεται ὁδὸν πρὸ προσώπου μου

To begin with, the first line of the citation in Matthew is identical to the Exodus passage in the LXX.[2] On the other hand, the word ἐξαποστέλλω from the Malachi passage is not found in the gospel citation. Moreover, the phrase πρὸ προσώπου σου, found in the gospels, is lacking in the first line of the Malachi passage, although the slightly different form, πρὸ προσώπου μου, is found at the end of the second line. The second line of the gospel citation bears only faint resemblance to the second line of the Malachi passage in the LXX, namely the word ὁδόν. Clearly the Septuagint of Malachi was not a source for our quotation.

Was, then, the MT for Mal 3:1 the source of the gospel citation, or of a part of it? It reads:

הִנְנִי שֹׁלֵחַ מַלְאָכִי וּפִנָּה־דֶרֶךְ לְפָנָי

---

[1] Indeed, Holtzmann (*Die synoptischen Evangelien* , 261) sees the whole citation as coming from Mal 3:1. Gundry claims that the second part of the citation shows only "a very slight influence from the Hebrew text of Mal 3:1" (*The Use of the Old Testament* , 11).

[2] Gundry (*The Use of the Old Testament* , 11, n. 2) wonders why only slight influence is seen from the Exodus passage, and so much influence attributed to the Malachi passage: "Why then should we see only a slight influence from Ex 23:20, with many commentators, when the whole first clause agrees word for word with Ex 23:20 LXX?"

Stendahl thinks that the MT and LXX texts differ, and uses this perceived difference to show that the gospel citation has been derived from the Hebrew text rather than the LXX.[1] He notes that the gospels' use of κατασκευάσει assumes the MT reading of פנה in the *piel*, while the LXX reads the *qal*, "for which reason the Synoptics' dependence on the Hebrew text is obvious."[2] That the gospel quotation adds a possessive pronoun after ὁδόν and (in Matthew and Luke) changes the Hebrew "before me" to "before you" can be explained by the need to adapt the OT quotation to its context in the gospels.

Stendahl's argument is based on the assumption that the Malachi passage was the basis for the gospel citation. To be consistent he then must interpret the gospels' use of κατασκευάσει rather than the LXX's ἐπιβλέψεται as Hebrew influence in the citation. While this goes against

---

[1]It appears that Gundry has simply followed Stendahl's line of argument in that, while he opts for the use of the Exodus passage over the Malachi passage, he does concede "a very slight influence from the Hebrew text of Mal 3:1" in the second half of the gospel citation (*The Use of the Old Testament* , 11).

[2]*The School* , 51. Stendahl's reason for saying that the LXX reads the *qal* here is the observation that "ἐπιβλέπειν is the usual rendering of פנה in the *qal* in the LXX." The difference here is only with the pointing of the Hebrew, so that the consonantal text is ambiguous without an oral tradition to interpret it. The MT interprets with the *piel* pointing.

Other recensions of the Greek have interpreted the verb פנה differently, showing that this word was problematic. Stendahl implies that Aquila's σχολάσει, Symmachus' ἀποσκευάσει, and Theodotion's ἑτοιμάσει all assume the *piel* reading. (The Göttingen LXX has the following: Aquila, ἀποσκευάσει; Symmachus, σχολάζει; Theodotion, ἑτοιμάζει.) Gundry states that ἀποσκευάσει and ἑτοιμάσει are based on the *piel* (*The Use of the Old Testament* , 11). He makes no mention of σχολάζει, suggesting that, in contrast to Stendahl, whom otherwise he appears to be following (like Stendahl he too assigns ἀποσκευάσει to Symmachus), he does not think σχολάζει is based on the *piel* . The verb σχολάζει can have the meaning of "devoting oneself to." This is much like the meaning of the *qal* (MT) of פנה in 2 Sam 9:8, "to concern oneself with."

In 2 Sam 9:8 the *qal* (MT) of פנה is translated by the LXX as ἐπιβλέπειν ("look upon"). Here it makes sense, although it is a literal translation. In Mal 3:1 ἐπιβλέπειν, if it means "look upon," makes little sense. The alternative, of course, is that ἐπιβλέπειν does not mean "look upon" but something like "concern oneself with" or "devote oneself to." In this case, ἐπιβλέπειν would make sense in both the Samuel and Malachi passages.

It is interesting that Mark (or his source) did not use any of the alternatives offered in Aquila, Symmachus, or Theodotion.

the gospels' use of the LXX which we have seen elsewhere,[1] there is always the possibility that Aramaic-speaking Christians who used the Hebrew text might have influenced gospel tradition at an earlier stage.

The MT of Mal 3:1 may, then, have been at the root of the gospel citation. It is at least not likely that the second part of the citation came from Exod 23:20. True, the τὴν ὁδόν of the gospels may reflect the τῇ ὁδῷ of the latter part of the Exodus passage, but this is not enough on which to build a case. Then whence came ὃς κατασκευάσει τὴν ὁδόν σου ἔμπροσ-θέν σου as found in Matthew and Luke, and ὅς κατασκευάσει τὴν ὁδόν σου as found in Mark?

The citation is introduced by a simple γέγραπται in Matthew and Luke. No prophet is claimed as the authority. Isaiah is claimed as the source in Mark, and this presents an obvious problem as this is simply not correct. To save face for the writer of the Marcan text, some, such as Holtzmann,[2] have suggested that the whole citation, ἰδοὺ ἐγὼ ἀποστέλλω τὸν ἄγγελόν μου πρὸ προσώπου σου, ὃς κατασκευάσει τὴν ὁδόν σου ἔμπροσθέν σου, was a late interpolation. While the suggestion of an interpolation is commonly made here, this should only be used as a last resort.

Because this citation does not fit into the regular pattern which Stendahl perceives, he makes an exception in this case and concedes that "it is reasonable to count on the possibility of testimonies,"[3] even though he launches a lengthy attack against the use of testimonies later in his book.[4] The problem with such a solution is that it solves nothing.

By suggesting the source is a testimony,[5] Stendahl indicates that the combination of the Exodus and Malachi texts predated the composition of

---

[1]Indeed, Stendahl himself asserts that "the quotation from Malachi is the only quotation common to the Synoptics which clearly shows influence from the Hebrew text," although he then mentions one other (*The School* , 52).

[2] *Die synoptischen Evangelien* , 261.

[3]*The School* , 51.

[4]*The School* , 207–217.

[5]Use of a testimony is the explanation to which many scholars resort in an attempt to deal with this very difficult passage, often as what they see as the only alternative to a later scribal insertion at Mark 1:2. Cf. Albright and Mann, *Matthew* , 136; C. S. Mann, *Mark: A New Translation with Introduction and Commentary* (Garden City, New York:

any of the gospels.[1] This seems reasonable. It is found in Christian tradition and shows up in both Mark's source and the source which Matthew and Luke used. It remains to determine what these sources were; in other words, what is the synoptic relationship here?

The form of the citation shows some differences over the three gospels. The pronoun ἐγώ is lacking in Mark (?) and Luke, and Mark lacks ἔμπροσθέν σου.

In terms of the Griesbach hypothesis the deletion of ἐγώ (it might have been in Mark) in Luke could be explained as simply a matter of style. The omission of ἔμπροσθέν σου in Mark could be explained in that the phrase is redundant after πρὸ προσώπου σου. The problem for the Griesbach position regarding this quotation is why Mark would omit the whole narrative common to Matthew and Luke, yet detach its quotation and insert it at 1:2.[2]

In terms of the two-document hypothesis the citation would appear in Mark (or his source) as it appears now. It would also appear in Q[3] but in a form including ἔμπροσθέν σου. This would explain the appearance of this phrase in both Matthew and Luke but not in Mark. In both sources, Mark and Q, ἐγώ would be lacking, perhaps because there is no reason for an emphatic personal pronoun here. Alternatively, ἐγώ could have been in Q but have been omitted by Luke on stylistic grounds. In conclusion, then, the evidence yielded by a study of this citation favors neither the two-document hypothesis nor the Griesbach hypothesis.

Doubleday, 1986) 195; D. E. Nineham, *The Gospel of St Mark* (Harmondsworth: Penguin, 1963) 60.

Others do not explicitly state the use of a testimony but suggest some early common Christian form. Ezra P. Gould asserts that the quotation is a free translation of the Hebrew, which appeared in "some common Greek source, not the LXX" (*A Critical and Exegetical Commentary on the Gospel According to St. Mark* [New York: Scribner's, 1903] 5). Willoughby C. Allen claims the quotation was current in Christian circles (*A Critical and Exegetical Commentary on the Gospel According to S. Matthew* [New York: Scribner's, 1907] 115.

[1] Gundry (*The Use of the Old Testament*, 11) claims that this combination was pre-Christian. Stendahl discusses such a possibility but rejects it (*The School*, 50).

[2] As we noted in our discussion of Holtzmann, the idea of a scribal insertion at Mark 1:2 has a long history. This possibility is kept alive in: Lagrange, *Saint Marc*, 4; Sherman E. Johnson, *A Commentary on the Gospel According to St. Mark* (London: Black, 1960) 33; Rawlinson, *St Mark*, 5.

[3] Davies and Allison concur (*Matthew*, vol.1, 294).

Matt 15:8-9

ὁ λαὸς οὗτος τοῖς χείλεσίν με τιμᾷ,
ἡ δὲ καρδία αὐτῶν πόρρω ἀπέχει ἀπ' ἐμοῦ·
μάτην δὲ σέβονταί με
διδάσκοντες διδασκαλίας ἐντάλματα ἀνθρώπων.

The preferred text for the parallel citation in Mark 7:6–7 differs from the Matthean text only in a small change in word order: ὁ λαὸς οὗτος] ουτος ο λαος.

The LXX for Isa 29·13 differs in the following ways from the preferred Matthean citation: ὁ λαὸς οὗτος τοῖς χείλεσίν με τιμᾷ] ἐγγίζει μοι ὁ λαὸς οὗτος τοῖς χείλεσιν αὐτῶν τιμῶσί με; διδάσκοντες διδασκαλίας ἐντάλματα ἀνθρώπων] διδάσκοντες ἐντάλματα ἀνθρώπων καὶ διδασκαλίας.[1]

The MT for Isa 29:13 reads:[2]

נִגַּשׁ הָעָם הַזֶּה בְּפִיו
וּבִשְׂפָתָיו כִּבְּדוּנִי וְלִבּוֹ רִחַק מִמֶּנִּי
וַתְּהִי יִרְאָתָם אֹתִי מִצְוַת אֲנָשִׁים מְלֻמָּדָה׃

The text of the LXX clearly differs from that of the MT. The whole syntactical relationship of v. 13 to v. 14 is different, and the smaller textual differences result from this major difference. In the Hebrew the words of the Lord begin with יַעַן כִּי ("because"). The rest of v. 13 is one long causal clause formed by a series of shorter coordinate clauses. The result clause (v. 14) is also long and composed of several shorter coordinate clauses. The Greek διὰ τοῦτο, which introduces v. 14, mirrors the

---

[1]Here Torrey (*Documents* , 70–71) sees a "two-fold process of contamination" in which the LXX assimilates to the NT and then the NT assimilates other parts of the quotation to the LXX.

[2]For כבדוני, *BHS* notes that 1QIsa[a] has כבדתי. I argue that this is a misreading of the scroll, in "The Confusion of ב–ו and ת, with Special Reference to 1QIsa[a] 29:13," forthcoming in *Revue de Qumrân* .

Hebrew לְךָ and so suggests a result clause such as that found in the Hebrew. R. R. Ottley suggests that in the case of μάτην the LXX translator read וּתֹהוּ ("in vain") for וַתְּהִי ("and is") and then altered the syntax by treating the following יִרְאָתָם as a verb to replace the lost one.[1] This mistake occurred because the ו and the י were difficult to distinguish.

The relationship of the MT to the LXX is problematic for this text but hardly unusual in the very free rendering of LXX Isaiah.[2] In the face of such great variation in the OT texts, the virtual equivalence of the Matthean and Marcan forms of the citation stands out all the more clearly. There are simply too many differences between the gospel citations and all known OT texts for any facile explanation of the origin of the citation.[3] Nevertheless, the gospel citations appear to have telescoped the two initial clauses of the LXX's rendition into one, and differ from the LXX in word order at the end. About all that can be said for sure is that the gospel citation is much closer to the LXX than it is to the MT.

The specifics in which the gospel text differs from the LXX version do not suggest in any obvious way that the citation might have been altered to fit better into its gospel context.

The only way in which the preferred texts of Matthew and Mark differ from one another with respect to this citation, the transposition of the first three words, ὁ λαὸς οὗτος / οὗτος ὁ λαός, does not offer any clue to the synoptic relationship here. If it is proposed that Matthew has corrected Mark toward the LXX, one might ask why only this phrase. Partial assimilation here is not impossible, but this is no sure indication of the priority of Mark. On the other hand, there is no reason to believe that Mark would alter what was in Matthew away from the LXX, in the absence of any other reason for the alteration.

[1]*The Book of Isaiah According to the Septuagint (Codex Alexandrinus)* ; vol.2: *Text and Notes* (Cambridge: Cambridge University Press, 1906) 250.
[2]Stendahl (*The School* , 58) finds no direct connection between the Hebrew and Greek texts, and virtually despairs at the abundance of variant texts for the latter part of the Greek verse. Gundry's attempt to make sense of a difficult situation assumes "corruption of the Hebrew text" and that the LXX has reproduced another form of the Hebrew (*The Use of the Old Testament* , 14–15).
[3]Albright and Mann suggest the quotation goes back to an "old Palestinian" tradition (*Matthew* , 184).

However, it could be argued that the Matthean context of the citation suggests a reworking of the order of the narrative better to incorporate the citation. As in Mark 1:1–11, Mark has the OT citation precede that which points to the citation. Immediately following the citation Mark writes, "Having neglected [ἀφέντες] God's commandment, you hold fast the tradition of men" (7:8). This summarizes the citation. Mark then virtually repeats v. 8 in v. 9 adding the sarcastic καλῶς, which serves to emphasize and add irony to the contrast set up in the citation between the worship of God and human teaching.

Just as in Matt 3:1–17, here also Matthew has not placed the citation first. The scribes and Pharisees have asked Jesus why his disciples do not wash their hands before they eat, thereby transgressing (παραβαίνειν) the tradition of the elders. Jesus immediately counters (v. 3), "And why do you transgress [παραβαίνειν] the commandment of God for the sake of your tradition?" Matthew's double use of the verb παραβαίνειν sets up an ironic parallel between the Pharisees' question and Jesus' counter-question, which emphasizes the contrast between the worship of God and the human teaching. Instead of a mere neglect (ἀφιέναι) of God's commandments as in Mark, Matthew has the transgression (παραβαίνειν) of God's commandments — moreover, the transgression of God's commandments *in order* to fulfil Pharisaic tradition. Matthew then uses the example of breaking God's commandment to honor father and mother, which Mark gives after the citation. Following this example of how Pharisaic tradition has transgressed God's commandment, Matthew has Jesus say, "You hypocrites! Well did Isaiah prophesy of you ... ," and concludes with the citation. Here the citation provides a forceful, emphatic way of finishing the lesson and rounds it out by pointing back to the gist of the citation which was given in v. 3.

Matthew's compact form of the narrative and his artful placement of the citation seem to drive home its point better than does Mark's rendition. It is unlikely, then, that Mark would have altered Matthew's version to a less artful form. This favors the two-document hypothesis.[1]

---

[1]It is to be noted here that we have not said that Matthew reworked Mark's version. This is where Holtzmann's form of the two-document hypothesis, with its *Urmarcus* , has a

Matt 22:32

ἐγώ εἰμι ὁ θεὸς Ἀβραὰμ καὶ ὁ θεὸς Ἰσαὰκ καὶ ὁ θεὸς Ἰακώβ;

The parallel citation in Mark 12:26 in the preferred text differs from Matthew in one way: εἰμι is omitted.

One variant reading is of interest: the last two ὁ's are included in ℵ A C L Θ Ψ f¹ f¹³ M ; Epiph, but omitted in B D W.

This variant text poses a problem, as indicated by the fact that Nestle-Aland had preferred text and variant reversed until the twenty-sixth edition. Even in the latter edition square brackets around the last two articles indicate indecision on the part of the editors. Their indecision is not unwarranted. The two proto-Alexandrian witnesses, ℵ and B are split. The preferred text has more Caesarean witnesses (Θ f¹ f¹³) than the variant (W), and the Koine group. Earlier editions of Nestle-Aland suggested that inclusion of the articles was the result of assimilation to the Matthean text.[1] Hence, there is no basis for clear resolution of this text.

The parallel passage in Luke 20:37 is not a direct citation but an allusion. Luke writes, "In the passage about the bush, where he [Moses] calls the Lord the God of Abraham, and the God of Isaac, and the God of Jacob." This indirect reference requires certain changes of case:

τὸν θεὸν Ἀβραὰμ καὶ θεὸν Ἰσαὰκ καὶ θεὸν Ἰακώβ

The LXX for Exod 3:6 reads:

---

distinct advantage over the form in which Mark is used directly by Matthew. Though Matthew's narrative is more artful than that of Mark, this does not necessarily imply that Matthew used Mark directly. All that can be concluded is that Matthew is more artful than Mark in his rendition of the narrative, and that Mark, who we would hope is at least artful enough to recognize good art in Matthew when he sees it, could not have used Matthew. Mark could easily have come later than Matthew, but simply not have made as artful a use of their common source.

[1] Codex ℵ is the only manuscript which omits these articles in Matthew, yet it has the articles in Mark. B D and W have the articles in Matthew, but lack them in Mark. For a similar case of non-assimilation within specific codices, see David S. New, "The Occurrence of αὐτῶν in Matthew 13.15 and the Process of Text Assimilation," *NTS* 37 (1991) 478–80.

ἐγώ εἰμι ὁ θεὸς τοῦ πατρός σου, θεὸς ᾽Αβραὰμ καὶ θεὸς
᾽Ισαὰκ καὶ θεὸς ᾽Ιακώβ.

The MT for Exod 3:6 reads:

אָנֹכִי אֱלֹהֵי אָבִיךָ אֱלֹהֵי אַבְרָהָם אֱלֹהֵי יִצְחָק וֵאלֹהֵי יַעֲקֹב

BHS cites a variation in some Hebrew manuscripts: אֱלֹהֵי [3°
וֵאלֹהֵי some Hebrew manuscripts, the Samaritan Pentateuch, the LXX.

That the LXX εἰμί has no correspondent word in the Hebrew
reflects simply a stylistic change in the Greek. The two texts can be
regarded as equivalent here. The phrase τοῦ πατρός σου in the singular
corresponds to the Hebrew text. As for the καί after ᾽Αβραάμ, all that can
be said is that some Greek manuscripts of Origen's time had the
conjunction, while Origen's Hebrew manuscript did not. More important is
that this is a formulaic saying which seems to be rendered consistently
within a given witness (cf. vv. 15, 16; 4:5). The use of the conjunction is
then simply a matter of style. Overall, then, the LXX and Hebrew are
virtually equivalent. Because the Hebrew and Greek OT are virtually equivalent, one cannot say for sure which text was the source of the citation, but
common wording and usage elsewhere suggest the LXX.

The only hint regarding the synoptic relationship is the verb εἰμί. It
is unlikely that this verb would be removed if it appeared in the source of an
evangelist, but it might be added. This would favor the two-document hypothesis. Greek usage does not require the verb εἰμί here, but its lack in
Mark suggests that his source lacked the verb. This citation has a formulaic
character, and was probably cited frequently by early Christians. It is found
in Acts 7:32, for example, without εἰμί. Without the verb (the verbless
sentence), the citation indicated the timeless relationship of God to his
people, and more closely resembled the Semitic form. Gundry claims that
the present tense, whether expressed or understood, is necessary to the
argument concerning resurrection.[1] If he is right, this would be grounds for

---

[1]*The Use of the Old Testament* , 21.

Matthew adding εἰμί to the Marcan version. It is unlikely that Matthew corrected Mark towards the LXX because if Mark had the articles Matthew failed to remove them in accordance with the LXX, and if Mark lacked them Matthew added them against Mark and against the LXX.

The synoptic relationship is evident when the synoptic citation is compared to that in Acts. The synoptic version lacks the OT phrase which appears in the LXX as θεὸς τοῦ πατρός σου and in Acts with πατρός in the plural form. The synoptics use the article throughout, with the possible exception of Mark. Mark is not likely to have used Matthew and Luke and corrected them towards the LXX by omitting the articles, or he would also have retained εἰμί.

Matt 15:4a

τίμα τὸν πατέρα καὶ τὴν μητέρα

The preferred text of Mark 7:10a differs from its Matthean parallel in that σου is found after πατέρα and μητέρα.

The LXX for Exod 20:12 differs from the Matthean text in that σου appears after πατέρα.

The LXX for Deut 5:16 differs from the Matthean text in that σου appears after πατέρα and after μητέρα.

The MT for Exod 20:12 reads:

כַּבֵּד אֶת־אָבִיךָ וְאֶת־אִמֶּךָ

The MT for Deut 5:16 is identical to that of Exod 20:12.

The LXX of Deut 5:16 corresponds exactly to the text of the MT, but that of Exod 20:12 lacks a σου to correspond to the pronominal suffix of the MT's אִמֶּךָ. For this reason the text of Deuteronomy likely was the source of the gospel citation. Common wording and usage elsewhere favor the LXX as source. When so common a text is in question, the possibility that the text of the gospels did not come directly from the Bible but from liturgical or catechetical forms used in synagogue/church, must not be overlooked.

The citation in Mark is identical to that of Deut 5:16 in the LXX. Matthew differs in leaving out the possessive pronouns, perhaps for stylistic reasons. Whereas Mark credits the citation to Moses, Matthew calls it God's commandment. In both gospels the contrast between God's commands and human traditions is central. Thus, for Mark to talk of Moses confuses things by offering a hint of tradition. Matthew cleans this up by following the previous verse's reference to God's commandments. While it is possible that Matthew preceded Mark and Mark corrected Matthew towards the LXX, it is highly unlikely that Mark would alter Matthew to a less polished rendition. Therefore, although the evidence is not overwhelming, Mark probably preceded Matthew.

Matt 19:18-19

οὐ φονεύσεις, οὐ μοιχεύσεις, οὐ κλέψεις, οὐ
ψευδομαρτυρήσεις, (19) τίμα τὸν πατέρα καὶ τὴν μητέρα,
καὶ ἀγαπήσεις τὸν πλησίον σου ὡς σεαυτόν.

The parallel citation in Mark 10:19 has so many minor differences from the Matthean citation that it is cited in full:

μὴ φονεύσῃς, μὴ μοιχεύσῃς, μὴ κλέψῃς, μὴ ψευδομαρτυρήσῃς,
μὴ ἀποστερήσῃς, τίμα τὸν πατέρα σου καὶ τὴν μητέρα.

There are some significant variant readings: μὴ ἀποστερήσῃς (ℵ A B² C D Θ 0274 M lat syᵖ·ʰ co)] omitted (B* K W Δ Ψ f¹ f¹³ 28 700 1010 al syˢ; Ir Cl); μητέρα] μητερα σου (ℵ* C N W Θ 28 565 al it vgᵐˢˢ syˢ·ᵖ).

Whether the original Marcan text had μητέρα or μητερα σου is a difficult problem. The latter is well attested in a wide range of text-types: proto-Alexandrian (ℵ), Caesarean (Θ 565), Western (Old Latin). It has the advantage in that it is not an assimilation to Matthew and Luke or to

Exodus, although it could be an assimilation to Deuteronomy. Μητέρα is witnessed by the proto-Alexandrian B and the rest of the Alexandrian uncials and so is favored over μητερα σου. The assimilation picture is the opposite of what we have just seen. No clear decision is possible.

Whether or not the original Marcan text had μὴ ἀποστερήσῃς is also difficult.[1] The best witnesses, the proto-Alexandrian manuscripts, are split. Omitting the phrase are the two Alexandrian witnesses, Δ and Ψ. So there is good witness to an original text which lacks μὴ ἀποστερήσῃς. On the other hand, omission could simply signify assimilation to Matthew and Luke. It could also result if a copyist deemed it inappropriate in a list of the Ten Commandments.[2] For these reasons, while there is no clear decision, the text containing μὴ ἀποστερήσῃς is favored.

The parallel citation in Luke 18:20 reads:

μὴ μοιχεύσῃς, μὴ φονεύσῃς, μὴ κλέψῃς, μὴ ψευδομαρτυρήσῃς, τίμα τὸν πατέρα σου καὶ τὴν μητέρα.

Exod 20:12–16 in the LXX reads:

Τίμα τὸν πατέρα σου καὶ τὴν μητέρα, ... (13) Οὐ μοιχεύσεις. (14) οὐ κλέψεις. (15) οὐ φονεύσεις. (16) οὐ ψευδομαρτυρήσεις κατὰ τοῦ πλησίον σου μαρτυρίαν ψευδῆ.

One significant variant follows: οὐ μοιχεύσεις οὐ κλέψεις οὐ φονεύσεις] ου φονευσεις ου μοιχευσεις ου κλεψεις (A F M, a large number of minuscules, the Bohairic translation, the Syro-Hexaplar).

The variant has greater support among the uncials and other witnesses than does the text of Codex B. The Syro-Hexaplar, based on Origen's fifth column, follows the Hebrew and must be discounted here.

---

[1]Metzger gives the text here a "C" rating (*A Textual Commentary* , 105). A "C" means that "there is a considerable degree of doubt whether the text or the apparatus contains the superior reading" (xxviii).

[2]Metzger, *A Textual Commentary* , 105.

Against the preponderance of witnesses is the probability of assimilation to the Hebrew. The preferred text stands.

Deut 5:16–20 in the LXX reads:

τίμα τὸν πατέρα σου καὶ τὴν μητέρα σου, ... (17) οὐ μοιχεύσεις. (18) οὐ φονεύσεις. (19) οὐ κλέψεις. (20) οὐ ψευδομαρτυρήσεις κατὰ τοῦ πλησίον σου μαρτυρίαν ψευδῆ.

The MT for Exod 20:12–16 reads:

(12) כַּבֵּד אֶת־אָבִיךָ וְאֶת־אִמֶּךָ ... (13) לֹא תִּרְצָח : (14) לֹא תִּנְאָף : (15) לֹא תִּגְנֹב : (16) לֹא־תַעֲנֶה בְרֵעֲךָ עֵד שָׁקֶר :

The MT for Deut 5:16–20 reads:

(16) כַּבֵּד אֶת־אָבִיךָ וְאֶת־אִמֶּךָ ... (17) לֹא תִּרְצָח : (18) וְלֹא תִּנְאָף : (19)וְלֹא תִּגְנֹב : (20)וְלֹא־תַעֲנֶה בְרֵעֲךָ עֵד שָׁוְא :

The best place to begin discussion of the synoptic relationship is with Mark's use of μὴ ἀποστερήσῃς against Matthew and Luke. Metzger's text-critical analysis assumes the two-document position.[1] He proposes that it was found in Mark, and then deleted by Matthew and Luke because they considered it inappropriate in a list of the Ten Commandments. Gundry also assumes the two-document position in trying to determine the text.[2] As he sees it, since Matthew and Luke lack μὴ ἀποστερήσῃς, the words may have been lacking in the original text of Mark, but introduced from "the unregulated tradition."

The assumption of a position with regard to the synoptic problem in order to determine the text is just the sort of stance which the present research hopes to discourage. In this case some conclusion as to whether or not Mark has μὴ ἀποστερήσῃς must be be reached independently of, and

---

[1]Metzger, *A Textual Commentary* , 105.
[2]*The Use of the Old Testament* , 18.

before any attempt is made to determine the synoptic relationship for this quotation, rather than assuming a particular synoptic relationship in order to determine whether or not Mark has μὴ ἀποστερήσῃς, as do Metzger and Gundry.

Whence came Mark's μὴ ἀποστερήσῃς? It is not part of the biblical Decalogue. Stendahl's proposal that there were several forms of the Decalogue used for catechetical purposes is tempting.[1] He notes that the commandment not to defraud (ἀποστερεῖν)was well-known in Jewish ethical teaching, and found its way into the LXX in A F M and V in Deut 24:14. It would not seem unlikely, then, that such a strain would find its way into Mark.

Because the Decalogue was such a common piece, appearing even in the MT and the LXX in the two forms of Exodus and Deuteronomy, it would be poor method to put too much weight on any small details of wording or to look only at the biblical passages as sources for the gospel citation of the Decalogue.[2] The text of the Hebrew Nash Papyrus had liturgical, devotional, or instructional use. Likewise, the gospel citations of the Decalogue should perhaps be viewed from a form critical, rather than a strictly source critical, perspective. In this light, "citation" might not be the most appropriate word for the passages here under consideration. "Citation" implies citation of some *biblical* text.

How chaotic things become if we insist on a strictly source critical perspective with regard to this "citation" can be demonstrated simply by observing the order of the three commandments, "do not murder," "do not commit adultery," and "do not steal," as they are found in various biblical texts. Let these three commandments be labelled "a," "b," and "c," respect-

---

[1]*The School* , 62.

[2]Gundry (*The Use of the Old Testament* , 17–19) mentions "the varying forms which the decalogue took in catechetical use," and gives a detailed table illustrating this statement. He goes on to state that Matthew has deviated from Mark and the LXX and followed the order of the MT; that LXX^A once again has assimilated to the NT; that the case for the assimilation of LXX^A to the NT is bolstered by the fact that here papyrus 963 "not as usual, agrees with B against A." (Gundry implies, but does not explicitly state, that usually 963 agrees with A against B. Compare Wevers (*Text History of the Greek Deuteromony* , 54) who observes that there is no close relationship between 963 and any of the later text groups.)

ively. The MT has the same order for both Exodus and Deuteronomy, but this might only be the result of assimilation. The Nash Papyrus and Philo (b-a-c) could witness to an alternate form of the Exodus text which became assimilated to the order found in Deuteronomy. The order in the LXX for Exodus is b-c-a for the preferred text and b-a-c for codices A F M (the same as Philo and the Nash Papyrus). In Deuteronomy the LXX's order is b-a-c for the preferred text, but a-b-c for the codices A F M. With so many combinations in the LXX, and perhaps only covered over in the MT by standardization, it is possible that even the OT texts were influenced by the liturgical/catechetical genre.

If we do not insist on strictly source critical assumptions, we do not have to ask whether, for example, Luke got his order, which differs from that of Matthew and Mark, from $LXX^{A\ F\ M}$'s Exodus, or LXX^{B}'s Deuteronomy. We do not have to ask whence came the μή-plus-the-subjunctive form found in Luke and Mark (but also in Jas 2:11), against Matthew and all forms of the LXX, especially in view of the fact that Mark and Luke do not use the same order.

The importance of form critical concepts in the study of this "citation" having been noted, does anything remain to be said concerning the synoptic relationship here?

The use of μή with the subjunctive as found in Mark and Luke (also Jas 2:11) presents no problem.[1] This is an alternative grammatical form for expressing prohibition. Compare the LXX's use of οὐ plus the future indicative. Matthew uses the LXX's form. On the two-document hypothesis, he would have corrected Mark toward the LXX, whereas Luke simply used Mark. On the Griesbach hypothesis, Matthew's form would have been put into a preferable grammatical form by Luke, and then Mark, who had access to both Matthew and Luke, would have chosen the Lucan version.

Now the problem of order is added to that of grammatical form. Assuming that the order of the commandments is not overly important (the LXX has a different order in different books, and various manuscripts of

---

[1]Gundry terms this construction "unusual" (*The Use of the Old Testament* , 17). Again, he assumes the two-document position in the determination of his text.

the LXX have a different order in the same book, and the orders found in
the LXX seldom correspond to the order found in the MT, and the Hebrew
Nash Papyrus differs from the MT), any of the gospels could change the
order of the others, unless they were restricting themselves to the order of a
biblical text. If the use of the same grammatical form as that in the LXX
indicates that Matthew used the LXX, then why did he not use the order of
the LXX also? Stendahl suggests that he used LXX^A.[1] Matthew has the
order of the Hebrew, yet it is unlikely that Matthew translated the Hebrew.[2]
He usually follows the LXX's οὐ plus the future indicative in prohibi-
tions.[3]

  If to the above is added the other differences among the gospel
citations, the following is a possible scenario. Under the Griesbach hypothesis, Mark can refer to Matthew and Luke. He takes his order from
Matthew but corrects the grammar according to Luke. Luke had probably
changed the Matthean order to conform with the LXX. Mark sees that
Matthew has ἀγαπήσεις τὸν πλησίον σου ὡς σεαυτόν while Luke
does not. Luke likely left this out because it was not part of the Decalogue,
and Mark would probably reason the same way. Besides, both use this
citation in another place. The clause τίμα τὸν πατέρα σου καὶ τὴν
μητέρα is adopted by Mark in its Lucan form, perhaps because Exodus has
the single σου in the LXX. It is noteworthy that, while Luke and Matthew
use the same form of this citation here as they did elsewhere, Mark omits
the second σου as does Luke, which Mark included in his other use of this
citation. This strongly suggests Mark has copied Luke here. Under the
Griesbach hypothesis, then, a very complex citation can be explained as an
eclectic text in Mark.

  The scenario under the two-document hypothesis follows. Luke
changes the order in Mark to conform with that of the LXX, and deletes μὴ

---

[1] *The School* , 62–63.

[2] Stendahl states a general observation resulting from his work: "We will find that the
catechetical quotations of Matthew are LXX in form even where they occur in material
peculiar to the First Gospel" (*The School* , 63).

[3] Concerning this grammmatical construction, see David S. New, "The Injunctive Future
and Existential Injunctions in the New Testament," *Journal for the Study of the New
Testament* 44 (1991) 113–127.

ἀποστερήσῃς because it is not part of the Decalogue. Matthew alters the grammatical form towards the LXX but keeps the order of Mark. He too deletes μὴ ἀποστερήσῃς because it is not part of the Decalogue, and adds the common ἀγαπήσεις τὸν πλησίον σου ὡς σεαυτόν.[1] This leaves two problems. Why does Matthew omit σου from τίμα τὸν πατέρα σου καὶ τὴν μητέρα?[2] Perhaps this is simply a matter of internal consistency; the σου is not necessary in Greek. Why does Matthew adopt the grammatical form of the LXX but not its order? Perhaps he used a Greek text with the same order as the Hebrew.

In the final analysis, the two-document hypothesis has a slight edge over the Griesbach hypothesis here in that it makes better sense that Matthew and Luke would delete μὴ ἀποστερήσῃς than that Mark and Luke would delete ἀγαπήσεις τὸν πλησίον σου ὡς σεαυτόν because the latter was part of Jesus' Great Commandment.

Matt 22:37

ἀγαπήσεις κύριον τὸν θεόν σου ἐν ὅλῃ τῇ καρδίᾳ σου καὶ ἐν ὅλῃ τῇ ψυχῇ σου καὶ ἐν ὅλῃ τῇ διανοίᾳ σου·

Significant variations are: ὅλῃ τῇ καρδίᾳ] ολη καρδια (א* B W Γ Δ Θ 0107^{vid} 0138 0161 f^{13} 28 700 1241 *pm*); ὅλῃ τῇ ψυχῇ] ολη ψυχη (B W Γ Δ Θ 0107^{vid} 0138 28 700 *pm*).

There are strong witnesses for both the first variant (א [original hand] B 0138) and the text (L is an Alexandrian manuscript). The strongest witnesses (the proto-Alexandrian) are split, although the preponderance of Alexandrian witnesses support the text. Hence, the text cannot be decided, although the evidence favors the preferred text. The same applies to the second variant concerning the article.

The parallel passage in Mark 12:29-30 reads:

---

[1]Stendahl proposes a number of reasons why Matthew may have added this particular citation here (*The School* , 63–64).

[2]Having said that Matthew assimilates the first part of the quotation toward the LXX, and under the assumption that Matthew in general assimilates toward the LXX, Allen is puzzled as to why he lacks σου (*Matthew* , 209, lxii).

ἄκουε, Ἰσραήλ, κύριος ὁ θεὸς ἡμῶν κύριος εἷς ἐστιν, (30) καὶ ἀγαπήσεις κύριον τὸν θεόν σου ἐξ ὅλης τῆς καρδίας σου καὶ ἐξ ὅλης τῆς ψυχῆς σου καὶ ἐξ ὅλῆς τῆς διανοίας σου καὶ ἐξ ὅλης τῆς ἰσχύος σου.

The passage in Luke 10:27 reads:

ἀγαπήσεις κύριον τὸν θεόν σου ἐξ ὅλης τῆς καρδίας σου καὶ ἐν ὅλῃ τῇ ψυχῇ σου καὶ ἐν ὅλῃ τῇ ἰσχύϊ σου καὶ ἐν ὅλῃ τῇ διανοίᾳ σου, ...

Two variant readings merit discussion: ὅλης τῆς καρδίας (ℵ A C L W Θ Ψ f¹³ M lat)] ολης καρδιας (papyrus-75 B Ξ 0124 pc); καρδίας σου καί] καρδιας σου (papyrus-75 B).

Whether or not the article was originally in the phrase ὅλης τῆς καρδίας is the most difficult textual problem in this Lucan citation. Strong witnesses for the preferred text include the proto-Alexandrian ℵ and other Alexandrian manuscripts. Supporting the omission of the article are the proto-Alexandrian B and papyrus-75 which dates from the early third century, and two other fairly strong witnesses, Ξ and 0124. This split evidence perhaps slightly favors inclusion of the article. The same must be said for inclusion of the καί in καρδίας σου καί. A clear decision regarding these texts is not possible.

In the LXX, Deut 6:4–5 reads:

Ἄκουε, Ἰσραήλ· κύριος ὁ θεὸς ἡμῶν κύριος εἷς ἐστιν. (5) καὶ ἀγαπήσεις κύριον τὸν θεόν σου ἐξ ὅλης τῆς διανοίας σου καὶ ἐξ ὅλης τῆς ψυχῆς σου καὶ ἐξ ὅλης τῆς δυνάμεώς σου.

Significant among the vast number of variant texts is: διανοίας (B Mᵐᵃʳᵍⁱⁿ papyrus-963, several minuscules, the Bohairic version)] καρδιας (A F M V, and all other manuscripts).

Here again is an example of a liturgical text, the *shema*. [1] For this reason, there are a great number of variants.

The preferred text (B M^{margin} papyrus-963, several minuscules, the Bohairic version) of the LXX has διανοίας—ψυχῆς—δυνάμεως which we shall label a-b-c, regardless of orthographic differences within each of these terms. The variant text (A F M V, and all other manuscripts) has καρδίας—ψυχῆς—δυνάμεως (d-b-c). Alfred Rahlfs'[2] text is found as a variant in Wevers. Wevers notes that the phrase "with thy whole heart and with thy whole soul" is common in Deuteronomy.[3] The word καρδία is used in every case but this one. This suggests to Wevers that here the original translator "intentionally chose" διανοίας, and that the variant resulted from assimilation to the common wording.[4] Wevers also gives papyrus-963 pre-eminent value as witness to the original text, especially when it aligns with Codex B.[5]

The MT for Deut 6:4–5 reads:

שְׁמַע יִשְׂרָאֵל יְהוָה אֱלֹהֵינוּ יְהוָה אֶחָד׃ (5) וְאָהַבְתָּ אֵת יְהוָה אֱלֹהֶיךָ בְּכָל־לְבָבְךָ וּבְכָל־נַפְשְׁךָ וּבְכָל־מְאֹדֶךָ׃

In contrast to the confusing picture offered by the renditions of Deut 6:5 in the LXX and the gospels,[6] that of v. 4 is starkly clear. Mark has reproduced the LXX exactly.

Neither Matthew nor Luke uses Deut 6:4. In Luke's case, it would not fit his context. Did Mark add Deut 6:4 to the accounts he found in Matthew and Luke, or did Matthew and Luke delete this from Mark?

---

[1] Stendahl (*The School* , 73) suggests that for this reason one must be cautious about drawing conclusions concerning the influence of OT texts upon such NT passages.

[2] *Septuaginta: Id est Vetus Testamentum Graece iuxta LXX interpretes* ; 2 vols. (Stuttgart: Privilegierte Württembergische Bibelanstalt, 1935).

[3] *Text History of the Greek Deuteronomy* , 91–92.

[4] *Text History of the Greek Deuteronomy* , 59.

[5] *Text History of the Greek Deuteronomy* , 54, 55.

[6] Gundry concludes his account of this citation with the remark that "the confusion ... defies disentangling" (*The Use of the Old Testament* , 24). He simply lists what he sees as "numerous possibilities."

First, let us consider the issue in the light of the two-document hypothesis. The implication that the Lord was Israel's God (as in Mark) would be the type of statement that Matthew or Luke, going to the gentile world, might wish to downplay.

What is interesting is that both Matthew and Luke made the same deletion, if one is to suppose Mark was their source. Matthew and Luke lack the material of Mark 12:32–34, with the exception of the end of Mark's v. 34 which Matthew places in another pericope in his own text (v. 46). Not only do Matthew and Luke lack the same material, they also have the same wording against Mark in several places. Both, for example, have a lawyer (νομικός [although this is uncertain in Matthew's text]; compare Mark's εἰς τῶν γραμματέων) test (πειράζων, ἐκπειράζων) Jesus. This might suggest that this pericope is found in Q as well as Mark, and that Matthew and Luke conflated the accounts found in their two sources. Both would conflate in different ways. The question Matthew has the lawyer ask is different from the question asked by Luke's lawyer. The latter asks about how to inherit eternal life, similar to Mark's theme of the kingdom of God.

On the Griesbach hypothesis Mark would have added the citation from Deut 6:4 and vv. 32–34. Matthew has set out his material so the Pharisees and Sadducees are clearly seen as groups opposing Jesus. In Matt 22:15–22 the Pharisees try to trick Jesus in their discussions, in vv. 23–33 Jesus replies to a question of main concern to the Sadducees, resurrection, in vv. 34–40 it is again the Pharisees who test Jesus, and in vv. 41–46 Jesus reverses the roles and asks the Pharisees a question. The chapter ends with the statement that after that day no one dared ask Jesus any more questions.

Instead of dividing the material into the types of questions asked by the two opposing groups, Mark follows the theme of resurrection with questioning by one of the scribes who comes up during the discussion with the Sadducees. After the scribe has finished his discussion, Jesus tells him that he is not far from the kingdom of God.

The Griesbach hypothesis has the advantage of accounting for the occurrence of Deut 6:4 in Mark. It also can account for Mark's splicing talk about the law with that about the kingdom. As well, it can encompass wording common to Matthew and Luke against Mark.

The two-document hypothesis gets around the problem that Mark would have had to have taken the theme of eternal life from a passage in Luke located at some distance from the material common to Mark and Matthew. It is much easier to understand Luke picking up on Jesus' remark about the kingdom and expanding it into a narrative which he would use in an entirely different place.

Was the citation from Deut 6:4 added by Mark or deleted by Matthew? A detailed examination of the context was needed in an attempt to answer this, but no conclusive decision can be made. Both hypotheses explain some things; neither can explain every difficulty.

The citation of Deut 6:5 may be only an apparent citation of the OT. This is a passage which probably served in both liturgical and catechetical capacities. For this reason, and because Greek anthropological terminology does not lend itself to equivalent translation of Hebrew anthropological terms, a vast number of Greek alternative translations, which try to do the impossible, result. It would be a mistaken procedure to push any attempt to draw conclusions about the gospels' relationship to the OT texts in this instance.[1] A few remarks will serve to illustrate this.

Both Stendahl[2] and Gundry[3] see Mark's use of the preposition ἐκ as an indication of dependence on the LXX. Why would he use the preposition but not the nouns? And what could be said about Luke's use of both prepositions on either two-document or Griesbachian grounds?

The various nouns which express the modes of loving God and the order in which they occur is a notorious problem. The three gospels all have καρδίᾳ, ψυχῇ, and διανοίᾳ, in that order (d-b-a), although Mark and Luke

---

[1] Gundry concludes that "Mt goes directly to the Hebrew text" (*The Use of the Old Testament* , 24). His view is shared by Albright and Mann (*Matthew* , 274). Allen says Matthew assimilates to the Hebrew in his use of ἐν for ἐκ (*Matthew* , 241).

[2] *The School* , 73. Stendahl does not explicitly assert Marcan dependence on the LXX here. He writes, "Mark stands closest to the LXX with the preposition ἐκ in all manuscripts throughout the passage." However, his next sentence, "Mark alone gives the famous first sentence of the *shema* , there too adhering to the LXX text," implies Marcan dependence for the preposition.

[3] *The Use of the Old Testament* , 23.

include ἰσχύος to give d-b-a-e and d-b-e-a, respectively. All three eschew
the LXX's δυνάμεως, while including both of the two major LXX variants
καρδίᾳ and ψυχῇ. At the same time, all three follow the LXX exactly in the
words ἀγαπήσεις κύριον τὸν θεόν σου, despite the fact that the imperative would have been more common Greek than the future. Stendahl cites
Matthew's and Mark's use of "the synonyms καρδίᾳ and διανοίᾳ" as so
unlikely a form of the *shema* that Matthew must have copied Mark here.[1] In
reducing Mark's list to three clauses (as in the *shema*), Matthew has
omitted the wrong clause. Now he has two equivalents of לבב and none
for מאד. This alteration suggests Matthew's use of Mark.[2]

One final point argues for the two-document position and helps to
give it a slight edge over the Griesbach position. The favorable portrayal of
the scribe in Mark becomes the stereotypical hostile Pharisee in Matthew;
the reverse is almost inconceivable.

Matt 19:5

> ἕνεκα τούτου καταλείψει ἄνθρωπος τὸν πατέρα καὶ τὴν
> μητέρα καὶ κολληθήσεται τῇ γυναικὶ αὐτοῦ, καὶ ἔσονται οἱ
> δύο εἰς σάρκα μίαν.

The preferred parallel text in Mark 10:7–8 differs from the preferred
Matthean text in the following ways: ἕνεκα] ἕνεκεν; πατέρα] πατέρα
αὐτοῦ; καὶ κολληθήσεται τῇ γυναικὶ αὐτοῦ] καὶ προσκολληθήσεται
πρὸς τὴν γυναῖκα αὐτοῦ.

One variant in Mark deserves attention: καὶ προσκολληθήσεται
πρὸς τὴν γυναῖκα αὐτοῦ (D W Θ f¹³ M lat syᵖ·ʰ co [A C L N Δ f¹ al: :
τη γυναικι])] omitted (ℵ B Ψ 892* syˢ).

This variant is problematic, as evidenced by the fact that only with
the twenty-sixth edition of Nestle-Aland has καὶ προσκολληθήσεται πρὸς

---

[1]*The School* , 75–76.
[2]Cf. Allen, *Matthew* , 241.

τὴν γυναῖκα αὐτοῦ been considered the preferred text.[1] The reason for this is the coincidence of the two best witnesses to the original text, ℵ and B, as witnesses to the omission of καὶ προσκολληθήσεται πρὸς τὴν γυναῖκα αὐτοῦ. Favoring its inclusion are the later Alexandrian manuscripts D and L (these have the clause with τη γυναικι instead of πρὸς τὴν γυναῖκα). Minuscule 892 is also late Alexandrian. The fact that the original hand of 892 lacked καὶ προσκολληθήσεται πρὸς τὴν γυναῖκα αὐτοῦ and it was later added in the margin, probably indicates no more than that it was made to conform to the common Koine text. The clause stands because without it οἱ δύο (v. 8) would refer to the father and the mother.

Why would some manuscripts lack καὶ προσκολληθήσεται πρὸς τὴν γυναῖκα αὐτοῦ? Perhaps it was a scribal error, with the eye passing from καί to καί. This would be more likely in those texts which had μητέρα αὐτοῦ before the first καί. It is perhaps, then, no mere coincidence that two of the three uncials with the omission also have μητερα αυτου (ℵ and Ψ). Many later scribes might have corrected the text by inserting καὶ προσκολληθήσεται πρὸς τὴν γυναῖκα αὐτοῦ into their work where the text they were copying lacked it, in order to give proper sense to the verse (this may have been what happened in the case of the margin of 892). The addition would have been according to the LXX text or Matthew. Note that C and L have και προσκολληθησεται τη γυναικι αυτου in Mark and also in Matthew.

The preferred text of the LXX for Gen 2:24 differs from the preferred Matthean text in the following ways: ἔνεκα] ἔνεκεν; πατέρα] πατέρα αὐτοῦ; καί κολληθήσεται τῇ γυναικὶ αὐτοῦ] καὶ προσκολ-ληθήσεται πρὸς τὴν γυναῖκα αὐτοῦ.

One variant warrants discussion: μητέρα (third-century papyrus-907, a large number of minuscules, including all of Wevers' group b)] μητερα αυτου (Codex M [under the asterisk], third-century papyrus-911).

---

[1]Allen's Marcan text lacks this clause. Hence, he can see the clause καὶ κολληθήσεται τῇ γυναικὶ αὐτοῦ in Matthew as an example of Matthew's assimilation toward the LXX (even though the similarity is rough) (*Matthew* , 277). This underlines the importance of careful discussion regarding determination of the texts.

In M αυτου has an asterisk, indicating that it was added to a Vorlage which lacked it because the Hebrew has the possessive pronoun. Third-century papyri are split over the two alternatives. Wevers observes that LXX Genesis is relatively free compared with the Hebrew with respect to the possessive pronoun, that A rarely supports the shorter text in this respect, and that the evidence in general indicates the shorter text will be the original.[1] In addition, he notes that where the MT has conjoined nouns with both having the same pronominal suffixes, LXX Genesis tends not to repeat the pronoun for the second noun.[2] The preferred text is maintained because the variant is an assimilation to the MT.

The MT for Gen 2:24 reads:

עַל־כֵּן יַעֲזָב־אִישׁ אֶת־אָבִיו וְאֶת־אִמּוֹ וְדָבַק בְּאִשְׁתּוֹ וְהָיוּ
לְבָשָׂר אֶחָד:

The preferred text of Mark is identical to the preferred text of the LXX. The only place where the LXX does not follow the Hebrew exactly is the use of one αὐτοῦ for the two pronominal suffixes in the Hebrew אָבִיו and אִמּוֹ. The fact that even here Mark is identical to the LXX indicates that he (or his source) has used the LXX, rather than translating the Hebrew independently.

It is worth observing that Matthew does not follow the LXX as closely as Mark. However, he differs only in points of style. He uses the Attic ἕνεκα rather than the Ionic and Hellenistic ἕνεκεν.[3] He is consistent in omitting the αὐτοῦ after πατέρα as well as μητέρα. In Matt 15:4a the possessive pronouns are also lacking for πατέρα as well as μητέρα, whereas in the parallel to that citation, Mark 7:10a, πατέρα as well as μητέρα have the possessive pronouns. Here, as well, Mark followed the LXX exactly. This suggests that the omission of possessive pronouns in such cases may be simply Matthean style. The third point in which Matthew

---

[1]John William Wevers, *Text History of the Greek Genesis* (Göttingen: Vandenhoeck & Ruprecht, 1974) 190.

[2]*Text History of the Greek Genesis* , 198.

[3]Henry St. John Thackeray, *A Grammar of the Old Testament in Greek* ; vol.1 (Cambridge: Cambridge University Press, 1909) 135.

differs from the LXX is also one of style, the use of the simplex verb κολληθήσεται followed by the dative τῇ γυναικί instead of προσκολληθήσεται πρὸς τὴν γυναῖκα.

Nevertheless, Matthew is not closer to the Hebrew than either the LXX or Mark, and in the use of ἕνεκεν τούτου, instead of διό, for עַל־כֵּן, and the use of εἶναι ... εἰς ... for ... הָיָה לְ, instead of γίνεσθαι, he obviously has used the LXX text and slightly altered it for stylistic purposes. Did he get it from Mark, or did Mark correct Matthew's citation towards the LXX? Because the differences are only stylistic, there is nothing in the relationship between context and citation which helps in this decision. Mark's correcting Matthew towards the LXX might be reason for thinking that Matthew was prior here. On the other hand, Matthew may have changed the Marcan quotation for stylistic reasons. There is not enough here upon which to base a decision concerning the synoptic relationship.

Matt 26:31

> πατάξω τὸν ποιμένα,
> καὶ διασκορπισθήσονται τὰ πρόβατα τῆς ποίμνης.

The preferred parallel citation in Mark 14:27 reads:

> πατάξω τὸν ποιμένα,
> καὶ τὰ πρόβατα διασκορπισθήσονται.

The preferred text for Zech 13:7 in the LXX reads:

> πατάξατε τοὺς ποιμένας καὶ ἐκσπάσατε τὰ πρόβατα

Zech 13:7 in the MT reads:

> הַךְ אֶת־הָרֹעֶה וּתְפוּצֶיןָ הַצֹּאן

That Matthew and Mark have the future indicative πατάξω against
the LXX's imperative πατάξατε and the MT's imperative הַךְ, is probably
to conform to the NT context of the quotation. Jesus has just said that his
closest followers will fall away in accordance with (γάρ, ὅτι) the prophecy
given in the quotation. The use of the first person singular future indicative
in the citation would indicate that it is a prophecy, whereas the imperative
does not. Use of the singular τὸν ποιμένα by Mark and Matthew to refer
to Jesus, instead of the LXX's plural τοὺς ποιμένας, also makes better
sense in the NT context.

Since the rest of the gospels' quotation is either identical to the LXX
or can be explained as adaptation of the LXX to the NT context, the only
word which might present a problem for the gospels' use of the LXX is
their use of διασκορπισθήσονται instead of ἐκσπάσατε. Again this could
possibly be an adaptation to context. Not only does the meaning of διασκορπισθήσονται fit better, but an imperative (such as ἐκσπάσατε) would be
out of place here.

The gospels' use of the verb διασκορπίζειν is closer to the meaning
of the Hebrew וּתְפוּצֶיןָ than to the LXX's ἐκσπάσατε. Several LXX
variants (A-Q, the Lucianic and Hexaplaric recensions, the Catena group)
have some form of διασκορπίζειν, although only A and Q and the Syro-
Hexaplar have the same form of the verb as Mark and Matthew. This poses
a problem. Did the verb διασκορπίζειν work itself into the LXX variants
from the NT or did the gospels get διασκορπίζειν from some form of the
LXX differing from the preferred text?

With regard to the synoptic relationship, there are signs that
Matthew used Mark. He has added τῆς ποίμνης.[1] Τῆς ποίμνης would
emphasize the cohesiveness of the group while the leader is present,
contrasted to its dispersion without its leader. Matthew, after all, is usually
recognized as the evangelist most concerned with the church. On the other
hand, one can hardly imagine why Mark would delete this phrase from
Matthew.

---

[1]Allen, *Matthew* , 277, here again presses too hard the case for Matthean assimilation to
the LXX. He suggests Matthew added τῆς ποίμνης to assimilate to a LXX with A's
text. Instead, LXX^A has assimilated to Matthew.

The change of order from Mark's τὰ πρόβατα διασκορπισθήσονται to Matthew's διασκορπισθήσονται τὰ πρόβατα may have been a
change towards the order of the LXX. Mark may have changed the order
from the LXX originally in order to juxtapose shepherd and sheep. Whatever the explanation, this could certainly go in either direction, and cannot
help resolve the synoptic relationship.

Outside the citation itself, the context gives some clues to the
synoptic relationship. These clues are sharpened by their contrast to a
context which is remarkably similar in both gospels. Matthew has ἐν ἐμοί
(v. 31) which is lacking in Mark. This is parallel to the thought expressed
by Matthew's addition of τῆς ποίμνης. It draws attention to the fact that
the very reason the group exists is Jesus, just as the very reason there is a
flock is the shepherd. The irony is that this is the very reason the group will
break up that night. This draws a tighter relationship between the context of
the citation, Jesus' prediction that they will fall away, and the citation itself,
the prophecy concerning the shepherd.

Chapter V

Quotations Appearing in Only One Synoptic Gospel

Henry Barclay Swete observes that there are three "distinct quotations" which are peculiar to Mark.[1] His list of OT citations found in the synoptic gospels[2] indicates only two: Mark 9:48; 12:32. The third is hidden under Mark "12:29f." We have treated this citation as part of the citation under Matt 22:37. Mark 12:29 is part of a composite citation, the part which has no parallel in Matthew or in Luke. It cites the LXX exactly, and is not a fresh translation of the Hebrew.

Considering Swete's criteria for determining what will be counted a citation,[3] it seems strange that he has included Mark 9:48 and Mark 12:32. Unlike all the other citations in Mark (except Mark 10:6; 10:7–8), which had parallels in Matthew, in these two cases there is no introductory formula indicating that what follows is meant to be understood as a citation, nor is it clear from their contexts that they are intended as citations. As well, unlike Mark 10:6; 10:7–8, which are identical to the LXX, they fail Swete's final criterion, "verbatim" agreement with a passage in the OT. It seems appropriate, therefore, to classify Mark 9:48 and Mark 12:32 as allusions.

---

[1]*An Introduction to the Old Testament in Greek* (revised ed.; New York: KTAV, 1968) 391.

[2]*Old Testament in Greek*, 386–387.

[3]*Old Testament in Greek*, 382.

Swete lists Luke 2:23 as a formal citation found only in Luke, with Exod 13:12 as the OT passage cited.[1] He has defined "direct citations" as "those which are cited with an introductory formula."[2] In this case the introductory formula is present (καθὼς γέγραπται ἐν νόμῳ κυρίου ὅτι), but one would be hard pressed indeed to see Exod 13:12, as found in either the LXX or the MT, as the source of the citation. Many Bibles cite the reference as Exod 13:2, indicating that the source is not clear. Here again, however, the Lucan text does not correspond to either the LXX text or the MT text. There is a resemblance of subject matter, and some common words, but no more. Luke 2:23, then, presents the strange case of an allusion masquerading as a formal citation, by means of its introductory formula.[3]

Luke 4:18–19[4]

    πνεῦμα κυρίου ἐπ' ἐμὲ
      οὗ εἵνεκεν ἔχρισέν με
    εὐαγγελίσασθαι πτωχοῖς,
      ἀπέσταλκέν με,
    κηρύξαι αἰχμαλώτοις ἄφεσιν
      καὶ τυφλοῖς ἀνάβλεψιν,
    ἀποστεῖλαι τεθραυσμένους ἐν ἀφέσει,
    (19) κηρύξαι ἐνιαυτὸν κυρίου δεκτόν.

There are no significant variant readings for this text.
Isa 61:1–2 in the LXX reads:

---

[1]*Old Testament in Greek* , 386.
[2]*Old Testament in Greek* , 382.
[3]Krister Stendahl, *The School of St. Matthew and its Use of the Old Testament* (2nd ed.; Lund: Gleerup, 1968) 94, sees "only two quotations in the strict sense of the word" in the material peculiar to Luke; namely, Luke 4:18–19; 22:37. These are the other two listed by Swete, *Old Testament in Greek* , 383.
[4]The order of presentation of quotations in this chapter is as follows. First are the quotations peculiar to Luke, then those peculiar to Matthew. Shorter quotations and/or those which most closely resemble a known OT text are presented before those which are longer and/or the text of which does not closely resemble a known OT text.

Πνεῦμα κυρίου ἐπ' ἐμέ, οὗ εἵνεκεν ἔχρισέ με· εὐαγγελίσασ-
θαι πτωχοῖς ἀπέσταλκέν με, ... κηρύξαι αἰχμαλώτοις ἄφεσιν
καὶ τυφλοῖς ἀνάβλεψιν, (2) καλέσαι ἐνιαυτὸν κυρίου δεκτὸν

That part cited by Luke of Isa 58:6 in the LXX reads:

ἀπόστελλε τεθραυσμένους ἐν ἀφέσει

There are no significant variant readings for either LXX text.
In the MT the selected portion of Isa 61:1–2 reads:

רוּחַ אֲדֹנָי יְהוִה עָלָי   יַעַן מָשַׁח יְהוָה אֹתִי
לְבַשֵּׂר עֲנָוִים שְׁלָחַנִי ...
לִקְרֹא לִשְׁבוּיִם דְּרוֹר   וְלַאֲסוּרִים פְּקַח־קוֹחַ:
(2) לִקְרֹא שְׁנַת־רָצוֹן לַיהוָה

In the MT the selected portion of Isa 58:6 reads:

וְשַׁלַּח רְצוּצִים חָפְשִׁים

There are at least three possible sources for Luke's citation: a Hebrew
text virtually identical to the MT, the LXX, or a Greek text which has been
altered towards the Hebrew and may be a forerunner of the hexaplaric
tradition.

In the first clause, πνεῦμα κυρίου ἐπ' ἐμέ, Luke agrees verbatim
with the LXX. The LXX differs from the MT in using κυρίου only once.
Clearly, Luke has sided with the Greek over the Hebrew in this case.[1]

---

[1]The phrase אֲדֹנָי יְהוִה is not a common one in the Hebrew text. It appears six other
times, all in Deutero-Isaiah (48:16; 50:4, 5, 7, 9; 51:4). Four of these occurrences are
from one of the Servant Songs, in which the Lord God sustains and helps his servant. That
it should be used in the Hebrew in 61:1, wherein the Lord God has sent the speaker and
placed his Spirit upon him, would be consistent with its other occurrences.

In his use of οὗ εἵνεκεν Luke has followed the LXX without any trace of translations attested in Aquila, Symmachus, and Theodotion.[1] The same can be said about his lacking the explicit κύριος as subject of the verb ἔχρισεν.

Luke follows the LXX in his use of πτωχοῖς and has the LXX's ἄφεσιν against Aquila's ἄδειαν, and the LXX's καὶ τυφλοῖς ἀνάβλεψιν against the alternatives found in Aquila, Symmachus, and Theodotion. The many alternate translations here indicate the difficulty presented by the Hebrew text. The verb פָּקַח means "to open," but it is used in the context of "eyes" and "ears" (Gen 3:5, 7; 21:19; Dan 9:18; Isa 35:5; 42:20). Here it is used with אֲסוּרִים ("those bound"), rather than עֲוֵרִים ("the blind"), so that the LXX clearly deviates from the Hebrew, in contradistinction to Aquila, Symmachus, and Theodotion who use δεδεμένοις. Luke again follows the LXX.

Luke has reproduced the words from Isa 58:6 exactly as they are in the LXX, with the necessary grammatical change of the imperative ἀπόστελλε to the aorist infinitive ἀποστεῖλαι. Once again Luke does not use any of the alternatives presented in Aquila and Symmachus.

Luke has followed the LXX of Isa 61:2 in the clause καλέσαι ἐνιαυτὸν κυρίου δεκτὸν except for replacing καλέσαι with its synonym κηρύξαι. Here Luke may be mirroring the MT's double use of קָרָא. It is Luke's only agreement with the MT against the LXX in this citation.[2] There is no extant evidence from Aquila, Symmachus, or Theodotion here.

With this one exception, and this could be simply a matter of style, Luke has clearly followed the LXX. His failure to use any of the alternatives furnished by Aquila, Symmachus, and Theodotion, shows that he did not use an alternate Greek text. He did not himself translate the Hebrew,[3] or he

---

[1] In place of οὗ εἵνεκεν Aquila and Symmachus have διότι, and Theodotion has ἀνθ' ὧν.

[2] Stendahl (*The School*, 96) thinks the LXX used καλέσαι for variety, and that Luke did not need this variety because he had interpolated the citation from Isa 58:6.

[3] Traugott Holtz sees clear influence of the LXX in this quotation. Luke is quoting directly from a scroll of Isaiah (*Untersuchungen über die alttestamentlichen Zitate bei Lukas* [Berlin: Academic Press, 1968] 40–41). Alfred Plummer thinks Luke relied on his memory here and that his quotation shows the influence of other passages (*A Critical and Exegetical*

would not so consistently have come up with the same translation as the LXX when so many possibilties exist.

Luke 22:37[1]

καὶ μετὰ ἀνόμων ἐλογίσθη·

In the LXX the relevant portion of Isa 53:12 reads:

καὶ ἐν τοῖς ἀνόμοις ἐλογίσθη·

In the MT the relevant portion of Isa 53:12 reads:

וְאֶת־פֹּשְׁעִים נִמְנָה

Commentary on the Gospel According to S. Luke [5th ed.; Edinburgh: T. & T. Clark, 1922] 120).

[1]This citation is repeated verbatim in Mark 15:28. This verse is not included in the preferred text. Bruce M. Metzger, *A Textual Commentary on the Greek New Testament* (2nd ed.; New York: United Bible Societies, 1975) 119, gives several reasons why this choice for "the text is virtually certain": (1) the earliest and best witnesses of the Alexandrian and the Western types of text lack v. 28; (2) there is no reason why, if the text were present originally, it should have been deleted, while, on the other hand, copyists could have added the sentence in the margin from Luke, whence it came into the text itself; (3) Mark very seldom expressly quotes the OT. Here Metzger is referring to the introductory formula found in v. 28, και επληρωθη η γραφη η λεγουσα, which indicates that the following quotation has been fulfilled.

While the external evidence may slightly favor exclusion of this verse, Metzger's second reason is the one which really decides the case. This verse fits admirably into the Marcan context, whereas the pericope in which it appears in Luke is a strange one indeed. In other words, it would have made much more sense if the citation had appeared in Mark. But if this were the case, why would Luke remove it from its Marcan context and place it in such a contrived context? If it were found first in Luke, as would be the case under the Griesbach hypothesis, one could understand Mark deleting Luke's pericope and inserting the citation in the scene at the cross. However, it is important to note here that in Luke the citation is on Jesus' lips, whereas in Mark there is simply the statement by Mark that this scripture is fulfilled. It seems highly unlikely that Mark would take the words of Jesus and not reproduce them as the words of Jesus. It may be that reliance upon the sanctity of the two-document hypothesis has moved the locus of the discussion from the level of source criticism to that of text criticism, without first examining the possibilities of the former. Nevertheless, the deciding question remains: Why would any scribe delete the verse from Mark if the work he was copying had it?

In the absence of clear evidence to the contrary, it can be assumed that Luke did not translate the Hebrew himself.[1] The LXX and Aquila, Symmachus, and Theodotion have provided alternative translations of the Hebrew. In his use of ἐλογίσθη and ἀνόμων Luke clearly has followed the LXX, rather than reproducing an alternative translation such as is found in Aquila, Symmachus, or Theodotion. The differences which do exist between Luke and the LXX are simply a matter of style. Luke's use of μετά should not be misconstrued as evidence that he translated the Hebrew himself. Aquila, who characteristically gives stilted and slavishly literal renditions of the Hebrew, did not have μετά. Luke may have taken μετά from a modified Greek text.[2]

Matt 5:21

οὐ φονεύσεις·

In the LXX Exod 20:15 is identical to the Matthean citation.
In the MT Exod 20:13 reads:

לֹא תִרְצָח׃

Matthew has used the LXX here.

Matt 5:27

οὐ μοιχεύσεις.

In the LXX Exod 20:13 is identical to the Matthean citation.
In the MT Exod 20:14 reads:

---

[1]Nevertheless, Joseph A. Fitzmyer finds Luke closer to the MT than the LXX (*The Gospel According to Luke (X–XXIV): Introduction, Translation, and Notes* [Garden City, New York: Doubleday, 1985] 1432).

[2]Holtz believes Luke was true to his Greek text (*Alttestamentlichen Zitate bei Lukas*, 42–43).

לֹא תִּנְאָף:

Matthew has again used the LXX here.

Matt 5:38

ὀφθαλμὸν ἀντὶ ὀφθαλμοῦ καὶ ὀδόντα ἀντὶ ὀδόντος.

The relevant portion of Exod 21:24 in the LXX is identical to the Matthean citation.

In the MT Exod 21:24 reads:

עַיִן תַּחַת עַיִן שֵׁן תַּחַת שֵׁן

Matthew clearly uses the LXX here, rather than himself translating the Hebrew. This is made clear by his use of the accusatives ὀφθαλμόν and ὀδόντα. Matthew should have switched to the nominative case for his citation in its context, but he has retained the accusative case which is found in the LXX. In the LXX the accusatives are the direct objects of the verb δώσει in the previous verse (Exod 21:23).

Matt 5:43

ἀγαπήσεις τὸν πλησίον σου

The relevant portion of Lev 19:18 in the LXX is identical to the Matthean citation. There are no significant variants for this text.

The relevant portion of Lev 19:18 in the MT reads:

וְאָהַבְתָּ לְרֵעֲךָ

Matthew has used the LXX here.

Swete lists two other passages from the Sermon on the Mount as
formal citations of the OT: Matt 5:31, 33.[1] Stendahl understates the case
when he writes, "In Mt. 5:31 and 5:33 ... the textual relation to the O.T. is
somewhat of a problem."[2]

This is immediately evident when commentators scramble hither and
yon in search of the OT passage cited. For Matt 5:33, Swete cites Num 30:3
with the suggestion to compare Deut 23:21. Gundry[3] cites Lev 19:12 and Ps
50:14 (MT) (Ps 49:14 in the LXX) with the suggestion to compare Num
30:3 and Deut 23:22–24, and Stendahl cites Lev 19:12. For Matt 5:31, Swete
cites Deut 24:1 and, while there is no disagreement that this is the passage
cited, Stendahl asserts that "Matthew here deviates both from the LXX and
the M.T. to the extent of an allusion."

John C. Hawkins[4] lists these two verses with Matt 5:21, 27, 38, 43.
All occur in the Sermon on the Mount. Hawkins displays some hesitancy to
list these with the quotations from the OT, in his statement, "The prefixed
ἐρρέθη seems to mark these passages as intended to be quotations, so they
are placed here for consideration." Hawkins has counted the words which
the Matthean passages have in common with the LXX. Of the six passages in
the Sermon on the Mount, 5:21, 27, 38, 43 are identical to the LXX, with
two exceptions. In 5:38 the word καί appears in the middle of the citation.
We have not counted this as part of the citation itself, but as a conjunction
connecting two parts of the citation. Hawkins has counted this as a word *in*
the citation which does not appear in the cited passage in the LXX. The other
exception is that Hawkins has counted the words καὶ μισήσεις τὸν ἐχθρόν
σου as part of the citation in 5:43 because "grammatically they form part of
the quotation, though they are not found in the O.T." We did not count these
words as part of the citation because they are not a citation of the OT.

This raises an interesting issue. Recall that Swete listed Luke 2:23 as
an OT citation, but we determined that it was at best an allusion sharing some

---

[1]*An Introduction* , 387.
[2]*The School* , 137.
[3]Robert Horton Gundry, *The Use of the Old Testament in St. Matthew's Gospel* (Leiden:
Brill, 1967) 108.
[4]*Horae Synopticae: Contributions to the Study of the Synoptic Problem* (2nd. ed.;
Oxford: Clarendon, 1909) 155.

content with an OT passage and merely masquerading as a citation by means of its introductory formula. This shows that Swete considers an introductory formula of a certain type as sufficient for a passage to be a citation. He then goes on to include some other passages as citations which do not have an introductory formula. We would define a citation as a passage which definitely corresponds closely to a particular OT passage *and* which is intended as a citation, whether or not there is an introductory formula.

Under this definition, the words καὶ μισήσεις τὸν ἐχθρόν σου are not part of the citation in Matt 5:43. The introductory word ἐρρέθη ("it was said") probably should not be seen as having the force of γέγραπται. Moreover, where does the clause καὶ μισήσεις τὸν ἐχθρόν σου come from? Stendahl[1] suggests that such sayings existed in Jewish catechism and that the ethical statements of the scribes and the early church were not exact quotations from Scripture. He cites the Manual of Discipline from Qumran as an example of such a catechism.

Returning to Hawkins' statistics on the number of words in "citations" which are found in the LXX, we note that only a small fraction of the words in Matt 5:31 and 5:33 come from the LXX. In this way they are strikingly different from the four citations (5:21, 27, 38, 43) in the Sermon on the Mount. This suggests that we should not let ourselves be overly influenced in our thinking by the fact that all six passages are introduced with the word ἐρρέθη. The fact that there exists a difference of opinion as to what OT passage(s) is cited in 5:33 suggests that this passage should perhaps not even be graced with the designation "allusion," let alone "citation." Hawkins could not even decide how many words in this verse were common to the LXX.

The only part of 5:33 which has direct contact with Lev 19:12 are the words οὐκ ἐπιορκήσεις ("you [singular] shall not swear falsely"). The MT's וְלֹא־תִשָּׁבְעוּ בִשְׁמִי לַשָּׁקֶר ("and you [plural] shall not swear by my name falsely") is rendered by καὶ οὐκ ὀμεῖσθε τῷ ὀνόματί μου ἐπ' ἀδίκῳ ("and you [plural] shall not swear by my name unjustly") in the LXX.[2] In the same

---

[1]*The School* , 137–138.

[2]It is interesting to note that Wevers, who is very thorough in citing NT passages which have some resemblance to the words in a given LXX verse (in his volumes of the

manner the remainder of the "citation" in 5:33 merely hints at a connection
with Ps 50:14 (MT) (Ps 49:14 in the LXX).

Stendahl suggests that in 5:33 Matthew is using catechetical material
known to him.[1] The commandment not to swear falsely would be unusual
for early Christians, especially considering Jesus' command not to swear at
all. Stendahl claims that the commandment not to swear falsely is Judaic
catechism because it is also found in the Didache (2:3), in which "the imprint
of Jewish catechism is the greatest."

In 5:31 there is only the faintest of verbal contact with Deut 24:1. The
passage in Matthew refers to a commandment to issue one's wife a certificate
of divorce when one divorces her. In the OT passage the man writes (the
indicative, not the imperative) his wife a bill of divorce. The concern here is
what happens *after* a bill of divorce has been issued.

Matt 13:35

> ἀνοίξω ἐν παραβολαῖς τὸ στόμα μου,
> ἐρεύξομαι κεκρυμμένα ἀπὸ καταβολῆς [κόσμου].

In the LXX Ps 77:2 reads:

> ἀνοίξω ἐν παραβολῇ τὸ στόμα μου,
> φθέγξομαι προβλήματα ἀπ᾽ ἀρχῆς.

In this quotation we have adopted Albert Pietersma's suggestion[2] of
παραβολή instead of Rahlfs' (the Göttingen text) παραβολαῖς.

In the MT Ps 78:2 reads:

Göttingen LXX), has no such notation for Lev 19:12. This indicates not an oversight by
Wevers but that Matt 5:33 does not resemble Lev 19:12 at all.
[1]*The School*, 137–138.
[2]*Two Manuscripts of the Greek Psalter* (Rome: Biblical Institute Press, 1978) 46.
Pietersma argues his point on the basis of *lectio difficilior*. He suggests that
παραβολαῖς, which has such widespread attestation in LXX manuscripts, originated in
Matthew.

אֶפְתְּחָה בְמָשָׁל פִּי אַבִּיעָה חִידוֹת מִנִּי־קֶדֶם:

With the exception of παραβολαῖς instead of παραβολή, Matthew
has the LXX text exactly for his first clause, ἀνοίξω ἐν παραβολαῖς τὸ
στόμα μου. Here Matthew has used παραβολαῖς to suit his context. Note
the plural form in the previous verse.[1] His use of the plural is against the
collective singular[2] מָשָׁל in the Hebrew.

With the exception of the preposition ἀπό, Matthew differs from the
LXX for the remainder of the citation. Nevertheless, ἀπό could signal LXX
usage; compare Aquila's ἐξ ἀρχῆθεν and Symmachus' lack of a
preposition.[3] Matthew might have used κεκρυμμένα because it better fits his
context than that of the LXX. In v. 11 he speaks of secrets and in vv. 13–17
he speaks of not seeing, just as we do not see something hidden. His use of
ἀπὸ καταβολῆς [κόσμου] would not only be consistent with v. 17, but
emphasize how far back in time these secrets have been hidden. Hence,
Matthew used the LXX but made some adaptations to his context, particularly in the second part of the quotation.

With regard to the synoptic relationship, the parallel passage in Mark
4:33–34 lacks an OT quotation. It is difficult to imagine what reason there
could be for Mark's omitting Matthew's quotation, so the two-document
hypothesis is favored here. Matthew appears to have added the quotation
himself as a reflection on the fulfilment of the prophetic word.

Matt 21:16

ἐκ στόματος νηπίων καὶ θηλαζόντων κατηρτίσω αἶνον

---

[1]*Two Manuscripts* , 46.

[2]The translation of the singular מָשָׁל as a collective singular would be quite natural,
especially considering its parallelism with the plural חִידוֹת. For the understanding of
singular words in Hebrew as collectives, see E. Kautzsch and A. E. Cowley, *Gesenius'
Hebrew Grammar* (Oxford: Clarendon, 1910) 394–396.

[3]Frederick Field, *Origenis Hexaplorum* , vol. 2 (Oxford, 1875) 224.

In the LXX the relevant part of Ps 8:3 is identical to the Matthean text.

In the MT the relevant part of Ps 8:3 reads:

מִפִּי עוֹלְלִים וְיֹנְקִים יִסַּדְתָּ עֹז

The LXX differs from the Hebrew. It may have been that the LXX translator found the Hebrew text so difficult to understand that he emended the text.[1]

Matthew has used the LXX here. The difficulty of the Hebrew makes possible too many other renditions for Matthew's identity with the LXX to be mere coincidence.

The context in which this quotation occurs is not found in Mark or Luke. This favors the two-document hypothesis. Why would both Mark and Luke omit this pericope if they found it in Matthew?

Matt 1:23

ἰδοὺ ἡ παρθένος ἐν γαστρὶ ἕξει καὶ τέξεται υἱόν,
καὶ καλέσουσιν τὸ ὄνομα αὐτοῦ Ἐμμανουήλ

The relevant part of Isa 7:14 in the LXX is identical to the Matthean citation with one exception: καλέσουσιν] καλέσεις.

The relevant part of Isa 7:14 in the MT reads:

הִנֵּה הָעַלְמָה הָרָה וְיֹלֶדֶת בֵּן וְקָרָאת שְׁמוֹ עִמָּנוּ אֵל :

Matthew has the LXX's παρθένος ("virgin") against the MT's הָעַלְמָה ("the young woman") and against νεᾶνις ("young woman") as

---

[1]Here he would have plenty of modern company. Gundry summarizes some examples (*The Use of the Old Testament* , 121).

found in Aquila, Symmachus, and Theodotion. Matthew's selection here obviously fits his context.[1]

Our evidence for Aquila, Symmachus, and Theodotion indicates that many alternative translations of the Hebrew are possible. In view of these possibilities, that Matthew has the LXX's wording clearly indicates that he used the LXX, rather than translating the Hebrew himself.

It should be noted that Matthew uses καλέσεις in v. 21 in a clause which almost parallels the citation, τέξεται δὲ υἱόν, καὶ καλέσεις τὸ ὄνομα αὐτοῦ 'Ιησοῦν. Here the verb is used in the sense of a personal command to Joseph. He obviously obeyed (v. 25). If v. 23 is also understood as a personal command, as would be the case if the MT is understood to mean "and she shall call,"[2] then Joseph did not obey. However, v. 23 is obviously not a personal command. It does not contradict v. 21 because the sense of v. 23 is "he will be acclaimed by the people as Emmanuel," and this sense is conveyed by the use of the third person plural impersonal καλέσουσιν as contrasted with the personal second person singular καλέσεις. Matthew's use of καλέσουσιν against καλέσεις as found in Aquila, Symmachus, and Theodotion and in the LXX reflects his need to make this change to be consistent with his context.

In conclusion, Matthew has used the LXX, except for καλέσεις. His use of the impersonal καλέσουσιν resulted from his own altering to suit his context.

---

[1]Ulrich Luz claims that Matthew normally quotes the LXX, unless he is following gospel sources, so this is not a special case for a special reason (*Matthew 1–7: A Commentary* [Minneapolis: Augsburg, 1989] 116).

W. D. Davies and Dale C. Allison suggest that in using παρθένος the LXX probably meant no more than she who is now a virgin will conceive and bear. Despite the fact that παρθένος usually translates בְּתוּלָה (except Gen 24:43), the LXX meant no miracle here (*A Critical and Exegetical Commentary on the Gospel According to Saint Matthew*, vol. 1 [Edinburgh: T. & T. Clark, 1988] 214). Willoughby C. Allen (*A Critical and Exegetical Commentary on the Gospel According to S. Matthew* [New York: Scribner's, 1907] 10) asserts that Isaiah meant עַלְמָה to have a sense of supernatural birth.

[2] וקראת is pointed as the second masculine singular or even the second feminine singular in some Hebrew manuscripts (Gundry, *The Use of the Old Testament*, 90, n. 4).

Matt 4:15–16

(15) γῆ Ζαβουλὼν καὶ γῆ Νεφθαλίμ,
ὁδὸν θαλάσσης, πέραν τοῦ 'Ιορδάνου,
Γαλιλαία τῶν ἐθνῶν,
(16) ὁ λαὸς ὁ καθήμενος ἐν σκότει
φῶς εἶδεν μέγα,
καὶ τοῖς καθημένοις ἐν χώρᾳ καὶ σκιᾷ θανάτου
φῶς ἀνέτειλεν αὐτοῖς.

The Matthean text has one significant variant: σκότει (א* C L Θ f¹ f¹³ *M*)] σκοτια (א¹ B D W; Or^pt).

Why was the variant considered the preferred text until the twenty-sixth edition of Nestle-Aland? σκότει was likely rejected as assimilation to the LXX. The present reasoning, in favor of σκότει, goes with the preponderance of witnesses, but it is a difficult decision. The text stands, but with the note that it cannot be definitely determined.

The relevant portion of Isa 9:1–2 in the LXX reads:

χώρα Ζαβουλων, ἡ γῆ Νεφθαλιμ ὁδὸν θαλάσσης ... καὶ πέραν τοῦ Ιορδάνου, Γαλιλαία τῶν ἐθνῶν, ... ὁ λαὸς ὁ πορευόμενος ἐν σκότει, ἴδετε φῶς μέγα· οἱ κατοικοῦντες ἐν χώρᾳ καὶ σκιᾷ θανάτου, φῶς λάμψει ἐφ᾽ ὑμᾶς.

While there are many variant readings for this text representing minor stylistic changes that have thin and scattered witness, none is of significance to our study.[1]

---

[1]Joseph Ziegler cites Isa 9:1 as a verse whose transmission is very uneven (*Septuaginta: Vetus Testamentum Graecum Auctoritate Academiae Scientiarum Gottingensis editum;* vol. 14: *Isaias* [2nd ed. Göttingen: Vandenhoeck & Ruprecht, 1967] 67).

I. L. Seeligmann proposes that the LXX translator, having difficulty with the Hebrew, obtained his description of the regions and districts of Palestine from Ezek 25:16 and the terms he used described the geography and the provinces of Palestine as they existed in his own time (*The Septuagint Version of Isaiah: A Discussion of its Problems* [Leiden: Brill, 1948] 74, 80).

The relevant portion of Isa 8:23–9:1 (including portions which are not cited in Matthew, in parentheses) in the MT reads:

(כְּעֵת הָרִאשׁוֹן הֵקַל) אַרְצָה זְבֻלוּן וְאַרְצָה נַפְתָּלִי (וְהָאַחֲרוֹן
הִכְבִּיד) דֶּרֶךְ הַיָּם עֵבֶר הַיַּרְדֵּן גְּלִיל הַגּוֹיִם:
(1) הָעָם הַהֹלְכִים בַּחֹשֶׁךְ   רָאוּ אוֹר גָּדוֹל
יֹשְׁבֵי בְּאֶרֶץ צַלְמָוֶת   אוֹר נָגַהּ עֲלֵיהֶם:

Here Matthew has extensively adapted the LXX to his context. The LXX is cast in the vocative and imperative but this would be unsuitable in Matthew's context of fulfilled prophecy so he has had to alter the LXX text. Nevertheless, Matthew's first verse, Ζαβουλων ... ἐθνῶν, is virtually identical to the LXX in that portion which he quotes.

In the second verse Matthew has altered the second person context of the LXX to suit his own third person context, just as he did in the first verse, but he has made some additional changes. He has substituted καθήμενος for the LXX's πορευόμενος and κατοικοῦτες, and ἀνέτειλεν for the LXX's λάμψει. Matthew has perhaps made these changes because sitting could suggest waiting. The people have waited in darkness (ignorance) for a savior, and now the sun has come up, the savior has come. Walking in darkness, as found in the LXX, suggests that the people have been sinful in their ways, a somewhat different emphasis.[1]

There is no evidence that Matthew has translated the Hebrew.[2] His first verse consists of a group of floating nouns. In the MT the two contrasting verbs הֵקַל and הִכְבִּיד syntactically tie these nouns down as

---

[1] The fact that this quotation can so easily be understood as an adaptation to Matthew's context makes gratuitous Georg Strecker's suggestion of the use of a testimony here (*Der Weg der Gerichtigkeit: Untersuchung zur Theologie des Matthäus* [Göttingen: Vandenhoeck & Ruprecht, 1971] 63–66).

[2] *Pace* Wilhelm Rothfuchs, *Die Erfüllungszitate des Matthäus-Evangeliums* (Stuttgart: Kohlhammer, 1969) 67–70, and Richard S. McConnell, *Law and Prophecy in Matthew's Gospel: The Authority and Use of the Old Testament in the Gospel of St. Matthew* (Basel: Friedrich Reinhardt, 1969) 119. Nor is there evidence in this quotation to support R. R. Ottley's conclusion that Matthew may have used a different LXX which was nearer the Hebrew than ours (*The Book of Isaiah According to the Septuagint (Codex Alexandrinus)*, vol. 2: *Text and Notes* [Cambridge: Cambridge University Press, 1906] 152–153). At no place has Matthew shown evidence of using a translation akin to that of Aquila, Symmachus, or Theodotion.

direct objects. No equivalent is found in Matthew. In addition, Matthew's use of καθήμενος and ἀνέτειλεν has no parallel in the MT.

This quotation appears to be an insertion into Mark 1:14–15 (Matthew's vv. 12, 17 are parallel to Mark's vv. 14, 15). Luke 4:14–15 does mention Jesus' return to Galilee and his teaching, but otherwise is not as close to Mark as Matthew. The quotation is peculiar to Matthew and illustrates the fulfilment of Isaiah's words. Because there is no apparent reason why both Mark and Luke would omit this quotation, if they found it in Matthew, the two-document position is favored here.

Matt 8:17

αὐτὸς τὰς ἀσθενείας ἡμῶν ἔλαβεν
καὶ τὰς νόσους ἐβάστασεν.

The relevant portion of Isa 53:4 in the LXX reads:

οὗτος τὰς ἁμαρτίας ἡμῶν φέρει καὶ περὶ ἡμῶν ὀδυνᾶται

There are no significant variant readings for either of these texts.
The relevant portion of Isa 53:4 in the MT reads:

אָכֵן חֳלָיֵנוּ הוּא נָשָׂא וּמַכְאֹבֵינוּ סְבָלָם

Outside of such relatively minor words as τάς and ἡμῶν, Matthew has no words in common with the LXX.[1] However, since Matthew's quotation is in the context of healing we might expect some adjustments to the LXX text. That Matthew interprets the bearing of sins, found in the LXX text, as the taking of infirmities presents no problem. Diseases and infirmities

---

[1] Some scholars can see no contact with the LXX for this citation. Cf. W. F. Albright and C. S. Mann, *Matthew: Introduction, Translation, and Notes* (Garden City, New York: Doubleday, 1971) 94.

There is no evidence that Matthew has used a translation akin to that of Aquila or Symmachus. Aquila has ὄντως αὐτὸς τὰς νόσους ἡμῶν ἀνέλαβεν καὶ τοὺς πολέμους ἡμῶν ὑπέμεινεν. There are several different citations for Symmachus in this instance.

were seen as the visible chastisement for earlier sins. Matthew's context mentions both the healing of the sick and the casting out of spirits. Moreover, that LXX Isa 53 has to do with the healing of physical ailment can be inferred from μαλακίαν (v. 3) and ἰάθημεν (v. 5). Matthew simply makes this more explicit. With respect to tense, Matthew uses the aorist, rather than the present tense of the LXX, but this is of no consequence since the LXX passage, apart from a sprinkling of the present tense, is set in the past. Hence, Matthew has used the LXX, with knowledge of its context, modifying its text to suit his context.

Parallel narratives in Mark 1:29–34 and Luke 4:38–41 lack the quotation but, unlike Matthew, include the statement that Jesus did not allow the demons to speak. Advocates of the two-document hypothesis would say that Luke followed Mark, and Matthew added the quotation to the Markan text. Advocates of the Griesbach hypothesis would say that Luke added the statement about the speaking of the demons to the Matthean text and deleted the quotation. Mark then followed Luke. They would have difficulty explaining why Luke would delete the quotation, however. Here the two-document hypothesis is favored.

Matt 12:18–21

(18) ἰδοὺ ὁ παῖς μου ὃν ᾑρέτισα,

ὁ ἀγαπητός μου εἰς ὃν εὐδόκησεν ἡ ψυχή μου·

θήσω τὸ πνεῦμά μου ἐπ' αὐτόν,

καὶ κρίσιν τοῖς ἔθνεσιν ἀπαγγελεῖ.

(19) οὐκ ἐρίσει οὐδὲ κραυγάσει,

οὐδὲ ἀκούσει τις ἐν ταῖς πλατείαις τὴν φωνὴν αὐτοῦ.

(20) κάλαμον συντετριμμένον οὐ κατεάξει

καὶ λίνον τυφόμενον οὐ σβέσει,

ἕως ἂν ἐκβάλῃ εἰς νῖκος τὴν κρίσιν.

(21) καὶ τῷ ὀνόματι αὐτοῦ ἔθνη ἐλπιοῦσιν.

There are no significant variant readings for this text.

In the LXX Isa 42:1–4 reads:

Ιακωβ ὁ παῖς μου, ἀντιλήμψομαι αὐτοῦ· Ισραηλ ὁ ἐκλεκτός
μου, προσεδέξατο αὐτὸν ἡ ψυχή μου· ἔδωκα τὸ πνεῦμά μου
ἐπ' αὐτόν, κρίσιν τοῖς ἔθνεσιν ἐξοίσει. (2) οὐ κεκράξεται οὐδὲ
ἀνήσει, οὐδὲ ἀκουσθήσεται ἔξω ἡ φωνὴ αὐτοῦ. (3) κάλαμον
τεθλασμένον οὐ συντρίψει καὶ λίνον καπνιζόμενον οὐ σβέσει,
ἀλλὰ εἰς ἀλήθειαν ἐξοίσει κρίσιν. (4) ἀναλάμψει καὶ οὐ
θραυσθήσεται, ἕως ἂν θῇ ἐπὶ τῆς γῆς κρίσιν· καὶ ἐπὶ τῷ
νόμῳ αὐτοῦ ἔθνη ἐλπιοῦσιν.

There are no significant variant readings for this text.
In the MT Isa 42:1–4 reads:

(1) הֵן עַבְדִּי אֶתְמָךְ־בּוֹ בְּחִירִי רָצְתָה נַפְשִׁי
נָתַתִּי רוּחִי עָלָיו מִשְׁפָּט לַגּוֹיִם יוֹצִיא:

(2) לֹא יִצְעַק וְלֹא יִשָּׂא וְלֹא־יַשְׁמִיעַ בַּחוּץ קוֹלוֹ:

(3) קָנֶה רָצוּץ לֹא יִשְׁבּוֹר וּפִשְׁתָּה כֵהָה לֹא יְכַבֶּנָּה
לֶאֱמֶת יוֹצִיא מִשְׁפָּט: (4) לֹא יִכְהֶה וְלֹא יָרוּץ
עַד־יָשִׂים בָּאָרֶץ מִשְׁפָּט וּלְתוֹרָתוֹ אִיִּים יְיַחֵילוּ:

In this quotation Matthew shows great variation from the LXX but
there are definite points of contact indicating that the LXX was his base. In
many places the LXX differs considerably from the MT but there is no
evidence that Matthew used the Hebrew.[1]

The LXX has 'Ιακωβ and 'Ισραηλ but Matthew clearly cannot use
these names as the quotation in the Matthean context is meant to refer to
Jesus. Hence, the fact that these names do not appear in the Hebrew cannot
be used to argue that Matthew used the Hebrew. That Matthew has παῖς
with the LXX rather than δοῦλος, as found in Aquila and Symmachus and
which the Hebrew would suggest, argues for a Septuagintal base, especially

---

[1]Albright and Mann conclude that either Matthew made a fresh translation of the Hebrew
or he used a different LXX (*Matthew* , 153). While this quotation differs considerably from
the LXX, there is no concrete evidence to support such a view. Matthew varies just as
widely, if not more so, from the Hebrew and other extant Greek texts.

since παῖς goes against Matthew's normal usage.[1] In his use of εὐδόκησεν against the LXX's προσεδέξατο Matthew may be hearkening back to the wording found in the narrative of Jesus' baptism (3:17). Here also is found ἀγαπητός, which is lacking in both the LXX and the MT. The baptism narrative also has God's spirit descending on Jesus. Here Matthew's use of τίθημι over the LXX's δίδωμι again is more reminiscent of the baptism, and Matthew's use of the future (θήσω) against the LXX's aorist (ἔδωκα) emphasizes that the words of the quotation are prophetic words. His ἀπαγγελεῖ ("proclaim") differs from the LXX and the MT ("bring forth").

For the next verse the LXX's οὐ κεκράξεται οὐδὲ ἀνήσει, οὐδὲ ἀκουσθήσεται ἔξω ἡ φωνὴ αὐτοῦ, is closer to the Hebrew than is Matthew. Again, Matthew has modified the LXX.

In the next verse Matthew departs considerably from the text of the LXX, but the LXX is closer to the MT than is Matthew. Again Matthew has altered the LXX, but shows no evidence of using the Hebrew.

Matthew's final verse does not render לֹא יִכְהֶה וְלֹא יָרוּץ עַד־יָשִׂים בָּאָרֶץ מִשְׁפָּט. This is translated in the LXX but somewhat loosely (a positive "he will shine out" for a negative "he will not grow dim," for example). The LXX's rendition of the final clause, וּלְתוֹרָתוֹ אִיִּים יְיַחֵילוּ ("the coasts will await his law"), is also quite loose ("and upon his law will the nations set their hope"), but it captures the thought of the MT.[2] In Matthew, by contrast, the focus of attention is not the law but the person of Jesus.[3] Matthew cleverly applies the LXX's ἔθνη ἐλπιοῦσιν to the name of Jesus, instead of the law. Here Matthew's purpose is clearly seen in his reworking of the LXX.

---

[1] Matthew has δοῦλος thirty times compared to eight times for παῖς (Robert Morgenthaler, *Statistik des neutestamentlichen Wortschatzes* [Zürich: Gotthelf, 1958] 90, 128). παῖς does not make Hawkins' list of words characteristic of Matthew (*Horae Synopticae* , 3).

[2] The Hebrew אִיִּים means "coasts, islands," but it is the Gentiles who live on the coasts and the islands; hence the association. Note, for example, the phrase אִיֵּי הַגּוֹיִם (Gen 10:5).

[3] In the Semitic world one's name implies the person.

Where Aquila, Symmachus, or Theodotion translate differently than the LXX, there is no evidence that Matthew has used a text akin to the text of any of these.

With respect to the synoptic problem, both Mark 3:7–12 and Luke 6:17–19 have a narrative parallel to that in which the Matthean quotation is found. Once again they lack the quotation, suggesting that Matthew inserted it into the narrative he found in Mark. Again the two-document hypothesis is favored over the Griesbach position because the latter would need to explain why both Mark and Luke omitted the Matthean quotation.

Matt 13:14–15

ἀκοῇ ἀκούσετε καὶ οὐ μὴ συνῆτε,
    καὶ βλέποντες βλέψετε καὶ οὐ μὴ ἴδητε.
(15) ἐπαχύνθη γὰρ ἡ καρδία τοῦ λαοῦ τούτου,
    καὶ τοῖς ὠσὶν βαρέως ἤκουσαν
    καὶ τοὺς ὀφθαλμοὺς αὐτῶν ἐκάμμυσαν,
μήποτε ἴδωσιν τοῖς ὀφθαλμοῖς
    καὶ τοῖς ὠσὶν ἀκούσωσιν
    καὶ τῇ καρδίᾳ συνῶσιν
    καὶ ἐπιστρέψωσιν καὶ ἰάσομαι αὐτούς.

There are no significant variant readings for this text.

In the LXX the relevant part of Isa 6:9–10 is identical to the Matthean citation except that the LXX has τοῖς ὠσὶν αὐτῶν βαρέως for Matthew's τοῖς ὠσὶν βαρέως.[1]

Variant readings found in Symmachus include: ἐπαχύνθη] ἐλιπάνθη (Symmachus [according to the margin of minuscule 710]); τοῦ λαοῦ τούτου ... ἰάσομαι αὐτούς] ὁ λαὸς οὗτος τὰ ὦτα ἐβάρυνε καὶ τοὺς ὀφθαλμοὺς αὐτοῦ ἔμυσε μήπως ἴδῃ ἐν τοῖς ὀφθαλμοῖς αὐτοῦ καὶ ἐν

---

[1]In codex ℵ the situation is the reverse: for the LXX the first hand of ℵ has τοις ωσιν βαρεως, and in Matthew ℵ has τοις ωσιν αυτων βαρεως. For an explanation of this phenomenon see David S. New, "The Occurrence of αὐτῶν in Matt 13.15 and the Process of Text Assimilation," *NTS* 37 (1991) 478–480.

τοῖς ὠσὶν ἀκούσῃ καὶ ἡ καρδία αὐτοῦ οὐ μὴ συνῇ καὶ ἐπιστράφῃ καὶ
ἰάθῃ (Symmachus [according to Theodoret]); the margin of 710 notes only
that Symmachus had καὶ τὰ ὠτὰ ἔβαρυνε).

In the MT the relevant part of Isa 6:9–10 reads:

שִׁמְעוּ שָׁמוֹעַ וְאַל־תָּבִינוּ וּרְאוּ רָאוֹ וְאַל־תֵּדָעוּ :
(10) הַשְׁמֵן לֵב־הָעָם הַזֶּה וְאָזְנָיו הַכְבֵּד וְעֵינָיו הָשַׁע
פֶּן־יִרְאֶה בְעֵינָיו וּבְאָזְנָיו יִשְׁמָע יְשְׁמְע וּלְבָבוֹ יָבִין וָשָׁב וְרָפָא לוֹ :

Matthew has clearly used the LXX here. His omission of an αὐτῶν
is consistent with his habit of erratically omitting possessive pronouns in
cases where they are grammatically and stylistically unnecessary. Matthew in
no place gives evidence of having used a text like that of Symmachus. The
text of Symmachus only makes clear that Matthew could not have arrived
coincidentally at the same translation as that of the LXX.

Stendahl views this exact duplication of the LXX with suspicion. He
claims that this citation was inserted at a later date.[1] As evidence he points
out that the same citation is given verbatim in Acts 28:26–27, with the
implication that someone copied the citation in Acts into Matthew. Why could
the copying, if any, not have gone the other way?

The citation fits its Matthean context admirably. In the parallel
passages, Mark and Luke use ἵνα plus the subjunctive in their allusion to the
Isaiah passage. As well as his formal citation, Matthew also has the allusion
parallel to that in Mark and Luke, but he has ὅτι plus the indicative. In
contrast to Mark and Luke, who use the allusion to explain Jesus' use of
parables, Matthew uses the allusion as a statement of facts which gives the
result of Jesus' speaking in parables. Matthew then uses the citation to show
that the facts given in the allusion are the fulfilment of the cited prophecy.
The interpolator would hardly have so altered Matthew's text.

---

[1]*The School*, 131–132. In view of Stendahl's classification of Matthew's citations into
two neat groups, the "*pesher* type" (introduced by the fulfilment formula), and the
"liturgical type" (p. 203), we might expect that he would have to devise some explanation
as to why this citation so obstinately refuses to fit his molds. For a counter-argument to
Stendahl, see Gundry, *The Use of the Old Testament*, 116–118.

It should be no surprise that Matthew can cite the LXX for the whole of such a long citation. If Matthew cites phrases of the LXX elsewhere (Matt 1:23, for example), why should he not on occasion do so more extensively? In other words, if the LXX passage fits, use it. The aorists ("this people's ... eyes have closed," for example) he finds in the LXX *do* suit Matthew's purposes, unlike the imperatives of the MT, so he uses them. So do the other features of the LXX translation.

Mark 4:10–12 and Luke 8:9–10 have a narrative parallel to that in which the Matthean quotation is found. They lack the quotation, suggesting that Matthew inserted it into the narrative he found in Mark.[1] Here the two-document hypothesis is favored over the Griesbach position because the latter would need to explain why both Mark and Luke omitted the Matthean quotation.

Matt 21:5

εἴπατε τῇ θυγατρὶ Σιών·
ἰδοὺ ὁ βασιλεύς σου ἔρχεταί σοι
πραῢς καὶ ἐπιβεβηκὼς ἐπὶ ὄνον
καὶ ἐπὶ πῶλον υἱὸν ὑποζυγίου.

There are no significant variant readings for this text.
In the LXX the relevant part of Isa 62:11 reads:

εἴπατε τῇ θυγατρὶ Σιων ...

In the LXX the relevant part of Zech 9:9 reads:

ἰδοὺ ὁ βασιλεύς σου ἔρχεταί σοι ... πραῢς καὶ ἐπιβεβηκὼς
ἐπὶ ὑποζύγιον καὶ πῶλον νέον.

There are no significant variant readings for this text.

---

[1]Allen believes Matthew uses the LXX to quote a passage suggested in Mark 4:12 (Matthew, 146).

Variant texts found in Aquila, Symmachus, and Theodotion include: πραὺς καὶ ἐπιβεβηκὼς ἐπὶ ὑποζύγιον καὶ πῶλον νέον] πραὺς καὶ ἐπιβεβηκὼς ἐπὶ ὄνου καὶ ἐπὶ πώλου υἱοῦ ὀνάδων (Aquila, according to Origen); πτωχὸς καὶ ἐπιβεβηκὼς ἐπὶ ὄνον καὶ πῶλον υἱὸν ὀνάδος (Symmachus, according to Origen; the margin of minuscule 86 notes only that Symmachus has ὄνον καὶ πῶλον υἱὸν ὀνάδος); ἐπακούων καὶ ἐπιβεβηκὼς ἐπὶ ὄνον καὶ πῶλον υἱὸν ὄνου (Theodotion, according to Origen).

In the MT the relevant part of Isa 62:11 reads:

אִמְרוּ לְבַת־צִיּוֹן

In the MT the relevant part of Zech 9:9 reads:

הִנֵּה מַלְכֵּךְ יָבוֹא לָךְ ...
עָנִי וְרֹכֵב עַל־חֲמוֹר וְעַל־עַיִר בֶּן־אֲתֹנוֹת:

That part of the citation which comes from Isaiah and the first clause of Matthew's citation from the Zechariah passage is identical to the LXX text.

The remainder of the citation, ἐπὶ ὄνον καὶ ἐπὶ πῶλον υἱὸν ὑποζυγίου, is clearly different from the LXX's ἐπὶ ὑποζύγιον καὶ πῶλον νέον. There is no evidence that Matthew translated the Hebrew. On the contrary, in v. 2 Matthew speaks of a female ass. All the words used in the Hebrew connote male animals, except אֲתֹנוֹת and this does not refer to an animal to be ridden by the king (it is in the absolute state, bound to the preceding noun).

Matthew modified the LXX text. He has the LXX's ὑποζύγιον, although not in the same place as the LXX; it is a word not found in Aquila, Symmachus, or Theodotion, and is a poor translation of the Hebrew.

Only Matthew, of all four gospels, has a narrative involving two animals. [1] That such a strange prophecy should come true, would all the more

---

[1]Rabbinic tradition speaks of only one ass. See Stendahl, *The School* , 119, 200.

show Jesus as the fulfilment of prophecy. Matthew omits the LXX's δίκαιος καὶ σῴζων ("just and a savior"), which one would have expected him to seize upon. This glaring omission suggests that the citation was given to emphasize something else, the two animals. Matthew's double use of ἐπί, against the single usage in the LXX, emphasizes the fact that Jesus rode both animals.

The narrative in which this quotation occurs in Matthew is found in Mark 11:1–3 and Luke 19:28–31, but without the quotation. The Marcan and Lucan versions have one animal, instead of Matthew's two. These similarities of Mark and Luke against Matthew are problematic for the Griesbach position, especially in light of the fact that Matthew appears to have reworked tradition and quotation to match each other. Here the two-document hypothesis is favored.

Matt 2:18

> φωνὴ ἐν ' Ραμὰ ἠκούσθη,
>   κλαυθμὸς καὶ ὀδυρμὸς πολύς·
> ' Ραχὴλ κλαίουσα τὰ τέκνα αὐτῆς,
>   καὶ οὐκ ἤθελεν παρακληθῆναι,
> ὅτι οὐκ εἰσίν.

There are no significant variant readings for this text.
In the LXX the relevant part of Jer 38:15 reads:

> Φωνὴ ἐν ' Ραμὰ ἠκούσθη θρήνου καὶ κλαυθμοῦ καὶ ὀδυρμοῦ·
> ' Ραχὴλ ἀποκλαιομένη οὐκ ἤθελε παύσασθαι ἐπὶ τοῖς υἱοῖς
> αὐτῆς, ὅτι οὐκ εἰσίν.

Variant readings found in Aquila, Symmachus, and Theodotion include: ἐν Ραμά] ἐν ὑψηλή (Aquila, according to the margin of minuscule 86); θρήνου καὶ κλαυθμοῦ καὶ ὀδυρμοῦ] μέλος κλαυθμοῦ πικραμμῶν (Aquila and Symmachus, according to the Syro-Hexaplar); the margin of 86 notes only that Aquila and Symmachus have πικραμμῶν; παύσασθαι ἐπὶ

τοῖς υἱοῖς αὐτῆς, ὅτι οὐκ εἰσίν] παρακληθῆναι ἐπὶ υἱοῖς αὐτῆς ὅτι
οὐκ εἰσίν (Aquila, according to the Syro-Hexaplar); the margin of Q notes
only that Aquila has παρακληθῆναι; the margin of 86 (under an asterisk)
notes only that Aquila has παρακληθῆναι; the margin of 86 (under an
asterisk) notes only that Aquila, Symmachus, and Theodotion have ἐπὶ τοῖς
υἱοῖς αὐτῆς.

In the MT the relevant part of Jer 31:15 reads:

קוֹל בְּרָמָה נִשְׁמָע נְהִי בְּכִי תַמְרוּרִים
רָחֵל מְבַכָּה עַל־בָּנֶיהָ מֵאֲנָה לְהִנָּחֵם
עַל־בָּנֶיהָ כִּי אֵינֶנּוּ׃

With the exception of φωνὴ ἐν ʽΡαμὰ ἠκούσθη at the beginning of
the quotation and ὅτι οὐκ εἰσίν at the end of the quotation, Matthew has
simply paraphrased the LXX. There is no evidence that Matthew used a
Greek Jeremiah similar to any of Aquila, Symmachus, or Theodotion. For
the LXX's three terms for mourning, all in the genitive, θρήνου καὶ
κλαυθμοῦ καὶ ὀδυρμοῦ, Matthew has two of them in apposition, κλαυθμὸς
καὶ ὀδυρμός and the modifier πολύς (note the different text for Aquila and
Symmachus here).

One similarity of Matthew's text to that of the Hebrew (לְהִנָּחֵם, "to
be comforted") is his παρακληθῆναι, found also in Aquila. However, there
are many dissimilarities. There is no equivalent for the second עַל־בָּנֶיהָ.[1]
There is no equivalent for תַמְרוּרִים (πολύς is too weak).[2] Particularly
against translation of the Hebrew is Matthew's use of τέκνα (which includes male and female children) rather than υἱοῖς ("sons"). If Matthew had
translated the Hebrew it would have been strange to use τέκνα when υἱοῖς
is just as possible a translation and more suitable in his context (Herod killed
the *male* children). In conclusion, then, it would be difficult to argue
convincingly that Matthew translated the Hebrew.

---

[1]The Hebrew text here is often rejected by modern OT commentators. See Gundry, *The Use of the Old Testament* , 96, n. 3.
[2]See M.-J. Lagrange, *Évangile selon Saint Matthieu* (Paris: Gabalda, 1927) 35.

Matt 2:15

ἐξ Αἰγύπτου ἐκάλεσα τὸν υἱόν μου.

There are no significant variant readings for this text.
In the LXX the relevant part of Hos 11:1 reads:

ἐξ Αἰγύπτου μετεκάλεσα τὰ τέκνα αὐτοῦ

In the MT the relevant part of Hos 11:1 reads:

וּמִמִּצְרַיִם קָרָאתִי לִבְנִי

As it stands the LXX would be unsuitable for Matthew's context.
Therefore, Matthew made the appropriate changes to the LXX text.

Matt 9:13; 12:7

ἔλεος θέλω καὶ οὐ θυσίαν

The relevant part of Hos 6:6 in the LXX is identical to the Matthean
citation. There are no significant variant readings for either of these texts.
The relevant part of Hos 6:6 in the MT reads:

חֶסֶד חָפַצְתִּי וְלֹא־זָבַח

Matthew has clearly used the LXX for this quotation.
In Matt 9:13 the emphasis seems to be on the first clause, ἔλεος
θέλω. Matthew's added γάρ in the following verse is inserted to connect the
thought of the two verses. Jesus came to call sinners, to offer, we must
infer, forgiveness. Hence, in *this* context, ἔλεος is an appropriate application of the more general statement of Hos 6:6.

In both cases of its use this citation appears in Matthew inserted into a narrative which has parallels in Mark and Luke.[1] This seems to favor the two-document hypothesis. It is difficult to imagine why both Mark and Luke would have left out these words of Jesus, especially when he is citing scripture, if they appeared in their source (*per* the Griesbach hypothesis). It is even more difficult to imagine why this would happen twice.

In addition, the citation's insertion into its context in Matt 9 is a little rough. The word "physician" from Jesus' statement in the previous verse, that "those who are well have no need of a physician, but those who are sick," connects directly with the subject of the words following the insertion, "I" (understood). Jesus is the physician. The parallelism between the two sets of clauses ("those who are well" with "the righteous," and "those who are sick" with "sinners") in the two passages on either side of the insertion might be missed if something were inserted between. Again, this favors the two-document hypothesis.

---

[1]Matt 9:13 occurs in a narrative (9:10–13) which has parallels in Mark 2:15–17 and Luke 5:29–32. Matt 12:7 occurs in a narrative (12:1–8) which has parallels in Mark 2:23–28 and Luke 6:1–5.

VI

Summary and Conclusions

Of the thirty-six OT citations examined, fifteen are found only in Matthew, two are found only in Luke, four are found in Matthew and Luke, six are found in Matthew and Mark, and nine are found in all three synoptics.

The vast number of citations peculiar to Matthew, when combined with the number of common quotations, would immediately suggest that Mark may have been the source of Matthew and Luke and that Matthew added these citations on his own, whereas Luke, who did not know Matthew's gospel, also lacked these. This is the reasoning that is often used in favor of the two-document hypothesis, in a general context, not specific to the OT citations. It rests on the question why Mark and Luke would have omitted so much of Matthew, if Matthew were the gospel used as the source of the other two. This argument can be transferred to this study and applied to the citations. It provides a problem embarrassingly difficult to handle for advocates of the Griesbach hypothesis.

There are no citations peculiar to Mark, unless one wishes to count Mark 12:29, which we included in our examination of Matt 22:37 and parallels. Here Mark quotes the LXX verbatim. Whether Matthew and Luke chose to omit this passage from their Marcan source, or Mark added it to what he found in his sources (Matthew and Luke), cannot be determined. However, under the two-document hypothesis it is possible for material to be common to both sources, Mark and Q. Here, on the two-document hypothesis, Mark would have a part of the quotation which Q lacked. In this single instance Matthew and Luke would both happen to have chosen to go with Q and omit the quotation.

As for the citations peculiar to Luke, Luke 4:18–19 is found in a context shared by the other synoptics, but only in the broadest of senses, while Luke 22:37 is in a context peculiar to Luke. Lucan quotations are not crucial to either the two-document or the Griesbach positions. There is never a need to explain why a Lucan quotation should be omitted in two gospels, as there would be for Matthean quotations under the Griesbach hypothesis, and for Marcan quotations under the two-document hypothesis.

With respect to the appearance, or non-appearance of quotations, then, the two-document hypothesis is clearly favored over the Griesbach position.

In their grouping of the citations peculiar to Matthew, Holtzmann, Stendahl, and Gundry have both merits and deficiencies.

Holtzmann is correct to say that for the most part Matthew has Septuagintal citations where these are found in Mark or Luke. On this point our study of the quotations goes further.

All four of the quotations common to Matthew and Luke are found in one location, the temptation narrative. This is in agreement with the general conception of Q. With the exception of Luke 4:11, which contains a few additional words from the quotation, and Luke 4:4 which omits a few words of the quotation, the Matthean and Lucan versions are identical. Moreover, Matt 4:10 and Luke 4:8 are identical but differ slightly from the OT passage, indicating a common gospel tradition which altered the LXX to suit the context of the narrative in which the quotation appears. In all four cases this tradition quoted the LXX, in two cases verbatim. This is consistent with the Q hypothesis.

Just as in the example of Mark 12:29, above, the view that Q and Mark can contain slightly different versions of the same narrative, proves useful in helping to resolve problems that troubled Holtzmann and others. Mark 1:2, for example, is combined with the following quotation in v. 3 in Mark and in pre-Marcan tradition. The two quotations, it is suggested, were found separately in two different narratives in Q. Matthew and Luke then simply chose the Q versions, rather than that of Mark.

In only four cases among those quotations common to Matthew and Mark or Matthew, Mark, and Luke (Matt 21:42 = Mark 12:10–11 = Luke 20:17; Matt 19:4 = Mark 10:6; Matt 22:39 = Mark 12:31 = Luke 10:27b; Matt 21:13 = Mark 11:17) is the LXX quoted verbatim. However, this small fraction of common quotations does not militate against Holtzmann's argument. All of the quotations common to Mark and Matthew or to Mark, Matthew, and Luke are basically Septuagintal. Indeed, Matthew is identical to Mark in three instances (Matt 22:44 = Mark 12:36; Matt 3:3 = Mark 1:3; Matt 15:4b = Mark 7:10b) in which their quotation differs from the LXX. Matt 15:8–9 and Mark 7:6–7 demonstrate similarity in the face of vast differentiation among known OT texts. Again, this indicates a common tradition.

Apparent correction of the quotation of one evangelist by that of another toward the LXX cannot be used as a criterion for favoring either the two-document or the Griesbach theory over the other. Twice Matthew appears to correct the other synoptics toward the LXX (11:10; 15:8–9), and twice Mark appears to correct the other synoptics toward the LXX (7:10a; 10:7–8).

This is particularly the case with Luke. Luke 20:42–43 appears to correct Matthew and Mark toward the LXX. However, Luke on his own apparently alters the LXX (3:5–6, despite the fact that in the first part of the same quotation, common to Matthew and Mark, Luke is identical to the other two synoptics in their closeness to the LXX; 4:18–19; 22:37).

Luke and Matthew dealt differently with their source(s). If we use the two-document hypothesis as reference, Luke's version is longer than that found in Matt 3:3 and 4:6, but shorter than that of Matt 4:4 and 21:42. Luke's wording differs from Matt 21:13 and he has an allusion where Matt 22:32 and Mark 12:26 have an explicit quotation.

Holtzmann is deficient in that he does not adequately treat the large number (at least seven) of citations peculiar to Matthew in which the LXX text is used. To preserve the division between the synoptic quotations, which are Septuagintal, and the quotations peculiar to Matthew, in which Matthew prefers the Hebrew text, Holtzmann separates off the four quotations found in the Sermon on the Mount as coming from a special Matthean source. He does not, however, fully recognize the other three Septuagintal quotations as peculiar to Matthew (21:16; 9:13 = 12:7; 13:14–15), preferring to see them as coming from source A, but receiving different treatment by Mark.

Stendahl separates those citations peculiar to Matthew into two groups: those introduced by the fulfilment formula (of mixed text-type), and those lacking this formula (use of the LXX). He thus corrects Holtzmann's deficiency (although he never specifically deals with Holtzmann's work).

Some adjustments may be necessary to Stendahl's neat division. We have argued that 13:14–15 has a formula much like that of Stendahl's formula quotations, yet it has a Septuagintal text. Stendahl claims this is a later insertion. Matt 1:23 is also a Septuagintal formula quotation. In addition, the first part of formula quotation 13:35 is identical to the LXX, and that part of formula quotation 21:5 which comes from Isa 62:11 is identical to the LXX.

Stendahl asserts[1] that Matthew has not simply translated the MT himself, but has used several OT sources, and interpreted these to suit his context. Our research suggests that this is not the case. On only three occasions did Matthew significantly alter the OT text to suit his purposes (4:15–16; 8:17; part of 13:35). On the contrary, there are two clear instances in which Matthew could, and perhaps should, have made alterations to his OT text to suit his purposes but did not (2:15; 2:18).

Gundry states that the citations peculiar to Matthew are of a mixed text-type, in contrast to the formal citations common to Matthew and Mark which alone are almost purely Septuagintal.[2] This should not be miscon-strued as meaning that all of the citations peculiar to Matthew are *individually* of a mixed text-type. Gundry later notes that seven of the quotations peculiar to Matthew are Septuagintal.[3] There is no reason, therefore, on the basis of text-type, to see the peculiarly Matthean quotations as a monolithic group. All fifteen quotations peculiar to Matthew which we examined were Septuagintal.

---

[1]*The School of St. Matthew and its Use of the Old Testament* (2nd ed.; Lund: Gleerup, 1968) 127.
[2]*The Use of the Old Testament in St. Matthew's Gospel* (Leiden: Brill, 1967) xi.
[3]*The Use of the Old Testament* , 149.

In our analysis of the quotations we have used textual data on the LXX some of which was unavailable to Stendahl and Gundry. Our observations indicate that Matthew followed his sources accurately, making only minor changes. Evidence for this is found in the fact that his quotations common with other synoptics are often identical in the face of a different LXX text. This indicates that Matthew may have used the other synoptic sources. We know that the direction of usage is from Mark to Matthew, and not from Matthew to Mark, through the results of our analysis of the common quotations with respect to their synoptic relationship. Here seven of these citations favored the two-document hypothesis on the basis of the wording of the quotations and an eighth favored the two-document hypothesis on the basis of the context of the quotation. None of the evidence clearly favored the Griesbach hypothesis, although eleven citations could be argued either way, favoring neither hypothesis over the other. Further evidence that Matthew follows his sources is his use of LXX texts against his purposes.

While the analysis of the synoptic relationship for the individual quotations may not be conclusive, evidence does favor the two-document hypothesis. Our observation concerning the care with which Matthew handles his sources should form a basis for further research on the synoptic problem.

Stendahl observed that a LXX tradition other than that now found in Codex B, among other sources, has been used by Matthew. Peter Katz suggests that one should not ask whether the quotations follow Codex A or B.[1] In the LXX no manuscript is homogeneous throughout. In the process of replacing scrolls by codices, the components need not have been of equal textual nature. The question which should be asked is: does a quotation follow a primitive or an edited text? Here is where our work has incorporated the findings of contemporary LXX research.

With regard to the OT text which was the basis for quotations in the synoptic gospels, we have found the LXX to be that basis throughout. We have proven mistaken Holtzmann's claim that, when on his own, Matthew

---

[1]"The Quotations from Deuteronomy in Hebrews," *ZNW* 49 (1958) 221–222.

preferred to quote from the Hebrew. Because we have found Matthew's OT to be the LXX, it is necessary to reject Gundry's assertion concerning mixed text-types with Semitic dimension and his explanation of these text-types. Similarly it is necessary to reject Soares Prabhu's conclusion that the LXX was not Matthew's Bible, that for a large number of quotations Matthew translated the Hebrew, adapting it to suit his context. At the same time our conclusion that the LXX was the basis of quotations found in all three synoptic gospels makes unnecessary Stendahl's theory that Matthew, as "targumist," composed his quotations from several OT sources.

Nevertheless, we are left with a few problem quotations which do not as cleanly fit our conclusion as we should like. Three quotations (Matt 12:18–21; 21:5; 26:31) show some similarity to the Hebrew against the LXX. These quotations are problematic both because of their similarity to the content of the Hebrew and because Matthew does not appear to have made these changes away from the LXX in order to suit his context. We have noted the accuracy with which Matthew follows his sources; the exceptions are those cases in which he has modified his source to suit his context.

Several theories have been used in the past to explain such cases: that Matthew translated the Hebrew; that Matthew used collections of quotations (testimonies) in use in his church; that Matthew relied on his memory, which in some cases played tricks on him; that Matthew used several OT sources for his quotations (Stendahl's "targumist"). In order to avoid such theories, some of which scholars have in general recently discredited, others which we claim to have discredited by this research, there is one possibility which ought to be considered.

Dominique Barthélemy has demonstrated the existence of first-century Greek texts of the OT which had been, in places, revised toward the Hebrew text.[1] The work of Dietrich-Alex Koch on the OT quotations in the Pauline epistles has shown the relevance of such findings for New Testament scholarship.[2] Hence, there is the possibility that the influence of a

---

[1]*Les Devanciers d'Aquila* (Leiden: Brill, 1963).
[2]*Die Schrift als Zeuge des Evangeliums: Untersuchungen zur Verwendung und zum Verständnis der Schrift bei Paulus* (Tübingen: Mohr, 1986).

LXX assimilated in places toward the Hebrew may have crept into some synoptic quotations.

Possible evidence is found in diverse strata of the synoptic tradition: the "formula" quotations of Matthew (12:18–21; 21:5), a quotation common to Matthew and Mark (Matt 26:31; Mark 14:27), and a quotation in Luke (3:5–6). In all of these cases the source is Septuagintal, but the gospel versions differ from our LXX, and display some similarity to the Hebrew. Because these textual discrepancies do not coincide with any obvious interest of the evangelists, some explanation is needed.

Let us make one point clear. This is merely an attempt to explain a few cases of textual anomaly. The paradigmatic case is use of the LXX by all strata of the synoptic tradition. We have no concrete evidence of the use of a LXX partially assimilated toward the Hebrew. This is simply a possibility proposed to offer an explanation for a few contrary quotations.

Bibliography

Primary Sources

Elliger, Karl and Wilhelm Rudolph, ed. *Biblia Hebraica Stuttgartensia* . Stuttgart: Deutsche Bibelgesellschaft, 1967–1977.

Field, Frederick, ed. *Origenis Hexaplorum* . Oxford, 1875.

Nestle, Erwin and Kurt Aland, ed. *Novum Testamentum Graece* . 26th ed.; Stuttgart: Privilegierte Württembergische bibelanstalt, 1979.

Rahlfs, Alfred, ed. *Septuaginta: Vetus Testamentum Graecum Auctoritate Academiae Scientiarum Gottingensis editum* ; vol. 10: *Psalmi cum Odis* . 3rd ed.; Göttingen: Vanderhoeck & Ruprecht, 1979.

Wevers, John William, ed. *Septuaginta: Vetus Testamentum Graecum Auctoritate Academiae Scientiarum Gottingensis editum* ; vol. 3.2: *Deuteronomium* . Göttingen: Vandenhoeck & Ruprecht, 1977.

_____, ed. *Septuaginta: Vetus Testamentum Graecum Auctoritate Academiae Scientiarum Gottingensis editum* ; vol. 2.1: *Exodus* . Göttingen: Vandenhoeck & Ruprecht, 1991.

_____, ed. *Septuaginta: Vetus Testamentum Graecum Auctoritate Academiae Scientiarum Gottingensis editum* ; vol. 1: *Genesis* . Göttingen: Vandenhoeck & Ruprecht, 1974.

_____, ed. *Septuaginta: Vetus Testamentum Graecum Auctoritate Academiae Scientiarum Gottingensis editum* ; vol. 2.2: *Leviticus* . Göttingen: Vandenhoeck & Ruprecht, 1986.

_____, ed. *Septuaginta: Vetus Testamentum Graecum Auctoritate Academiae Scientiarum Gottingensis editum* ; vol. 3.1: *Numeri* . Göttingen: Vandenhoeck & Ruprecht, 1982.

Ziegler, Joseph, ed. *Septuaginta: Vetus Testamentum Graecum Auctoritate*

Academiae Scientiarum Gottingensis editum ; vol. 13: *Duodecim Prophetae.* 2nd ed.; Göttingen: Vandenhoeck & Ruprecht, 1967.

_____, ed. *Septuaginta: Vetus Testamentum Graecum Auctoritate Academiae Scientiarum Gottingensis editum* ; vol. 15: *Ieremias, Baruch, Threni, Epistula Ieremiae* . 2nd ed.; Göttingen: Vandenhoeck & Ruprecht, 1976.

_____, ed. *Septuaginta: Vetus Testamentum Graecum Auctoritate Academiae Scientiarum Gottingensis editum* ; vol. 14: *Isaias* . 2nd ed.; Göttingen: Vandenhoeck & Ruprecht, 1967.

Secondary Sources

Aland, Kurt and Barbara Aland. *The Text of the New Testament: An Introduction to the Critical Editions and to the Theory and Practice of Modern Textual Criticism* . Grand Rapids: William B. Eerdmans, 1987.

Albright, W. F. and C. S. Mann. *Matthew: Introduction, Translation, and Notes* . Garden City, New York: Doubleday, 1971.

Allen, Willoughby Charles. *A Critical and Exegetical Commentary on the Gospel According to S. Matthew* . New York: Charles Scribner's Sons, 1907.

_____. "The Old Testament Quotations in St. Matthew and St. Mark," *ExpT* 12 (1900–1901) 281–283.

Barrett, Charles Kingsley. "Luke/Acts," in D. A. Carson and H. G. M. Williamson, ed., *It is Written: Scripture Citing Scripture* (Cambridge: Cambridge University Press, 1988) 231–244.

Bartnicki, Roman. "Das Zitat von Zach 9:9–10 und die Tiere im Bericht von Matthäus über dem Einzug Jesu in Jerusalem (Mt 21:1–11)," *NovT* 18 (1976) 161–166.

Barthélemy, Dominique. *Les Devanciers d'Aquila* . Leiden: E. J. Brill, 1963.

Baumstark, A. "Die Zitate des Mt.-Evangeliums aus dem Zwolfprophetenbuch," *Bib* 37 (1956) 296–313.

Bellinzoni, Arthur J., Jr., Joseph B. Tyson and William O. Walker, Jr., ed. *The Two-Source Hypothesis: A Critical Appraisal* . Macon, Georgia: Mercer University Press, 1985.

Blass, Friedrich, Albert Debrunner and Friedrich Rehkopf. *A Greek Grammar of the New Testament and Other Early Christian Literature.* Tr. Robert W. Funk. Chicago: University of Chicago Press, 1961.

Bleek, Friedrich. *Beiträge zur Einleitung und Auslegung der heiligen Schrift;* vol. 1: *Beiträge zur Evangelien-Kritik* . Berlin: G. Reimer, 1846.

Böhl, Eduard. *Die alttestamentlichen Citate im Neuen Testament* . Vienna: Wilhelm Braumüller, 1878.

_____. *Forschungen nach einer Volksbibel zur Zeit Jesu und deren Zusammenhang mit der Septuaginta-übersetzung* . Vienna: W. Braumüller, 1873.

Brown, Raymond E. *The Birth of the Messiah* . London: Cassell, 1977.

Butler, B. C. *The Originality of St Matthew: A Critique of the Two-Document Hypothesis* . Cambridge: Cambridge University Press, 1951.

Chester, Andrew. "Citing the Old Testament," in D. A. Carson and H. G. M. Williamson, ed., *It is Written: Scripture Citing Scripture* (Cambridge: Cambridge University Press, 1988) 141–169.

Coleman, R. O. "Matthew's Use of the Old Testament," *Southwestern Journal of Theology* 5 (1962) 29–39.

Cope, O. Lamar. *Matthew: A Scribe Trained for the Kingdom of Heaven* . Washington: The Catholic Biblical Association of America, 1976.

Credner, Karl August. *Einleitung in das Neue Testament* ; vol. 1. Halle: Verlag der Buchhandlung des Waisenhauses, 1836.

Davies, William David and Dale C. Allison, Jr. *A Critical and Exegetical Commentary on the Gospel According to Saint Matthew* ; vol. 1: *Introduction and Commentary on Matthew I–VII* . Edinburgh: T. & T. Clark, 1988.

Delling, G. "πληρόω," *TDNT* 6 (1968) 286–298.

Edgar, S. L. "Respect for Context in Quotations from the Old Testament," *NTS* 9 (1962–1963) 55–62.

Farmer, William R. "A 'Skeleton in the Closet' of Gospel Research," *BR* 6 (1961) 18–42.

_____, ed. *New Synoptic Studies: The Cambridge Gospel Conference and Beyond.* Macon, Georgia: Mercer University Press, 1982.

_____. *The Synoptic Problem: A Critical Analysis* . Dillsboro, North Carolina: Western North Carolina Press, 1976.

Fee, Gordon D. "Modern Text Criticism and the Synoptic Problem," in Bernard Orchard and Thomas R. W.Longstaff, ed., *J. J. Griesbach:*

128   Old Testament Quotations

Synoptic and Text-critical Studies, 1776–1976 . Cambridge: Cambridge University Press, 1978.

Fitzmyer, Joseph A. "The Priority of Mark and the 'Q' Source in Luke," in *Jesus and Man's Hope* , vol. 1 (Pittsburgh: Pittsburgh Theological Seminary, 1970) 131–170.

_____. "The Use of Explicit Old Testament Quotations in Qumran Literature and in the New Testament," *NTS* 7 (1960–1961) 297–333.

France, Richard T. "The Formula-quotations of Matthew 2 and the Problem of Communication," *NTS* 27 (1981) 233–251.

Gärtner, B. "The Habakkuk Commentary (DSH) and the Gospel of Matthew," *ST* 8 (1954) 1–24.

Gould, Ezra P. *A Critical and Exegetical Commentary on the Gospel According to Saint Mark* . New York: Charles Scribner's Sons, 1896.

Goulder, Michael D. *Luke: A New Paradigm* . 2 vols. Sheffield: Sheffield Academic Press, 1989.

Grindel, John A. "Matthew 12:18–21," *CBQ* 29 (1967) 110–115.

Gundry, Robert Horton. *The Use of the Old Testament in St. Matthew's Gospel* . Leiden: E. J. Brill, 1967.

Haupt, Erich. *Die alttestamentlichen Citate der vier Evangelien* . Colberg: C. Jancke, 1871.

Hawkins, John C. *Horae Synopticae: Contributions to the Study of the Synoptic Problem* . 2nd ed.; Oxford: Clarendon, 1909.

Heater, Homer. "Matthew 2:6 and its Old Testament Sources," *Journal of the Evangelical Theological Society* 26 (1983) 395–397.

Hill, David. "On the Use and Meaning of Hosea 6:6 in Matthew's Gospel (Hos 6:6; Matt 9:13, 12:7; Mk 2:13–17, 23–27)," *NTS* 24 (1977) 107–119.

Hillyer, N. "Matthew's Use of the Old Testament," *EvQ* 36 (1964) 12–26.

Holtz, Traugott. *Untersuchungen über die alttestamentlichen Zitate bei Lukas.* Berlin: Akademie Verlag, 1968.

Holtzmann, Heinrich Julius. *Hand-commentar zum Neuen Testament* ; vol. 1. *Die Synoptiker, Die Apostelgeschichte* . 2nd ed.; Freiburg: Mohr, 1892.

_____. *Lehrbuch der historisch-kritischen Einleitung in das Neue Testament.*

3rd ed.; Freiburg: J. C. B. Mohr, 1892.

_____. *Die synoptischen Evangelien: Ihr Ursprung und geschichtlicher Charakter*. Leipzig: Engelmann, 1863.

Hurtado, Larry W. *Text-critical Methodology and the Pre-Caesarean Text: Codex W in the Gospel of Mark*. Grand Rapids: Eerdmans, 1981.

Jellicoe, Sidney. *The Septuagint and Modern Study*. Oxford: Clarendon, 1968.

_____. *Studies in the Septuagint: Origins, Recensions, and Interpretations*. New York: KTAV, 1974.

Johnson, Sherman E. "The Biblical Quotations in Matthew," *HTR* 36 (1943) 135–153.

Kahle, Paul Ernst. *The Cairo Geniza*. London: Oxford University Press, 1947.

Katz, Peter. "The Quotations from Deuteronomy in Hebrews," *ZNW* 49 (1958) 213–223.

Koch, Dietrich-Alex. *Die Schrift als Zeuge des Evangeliums: Untersuchungen zur Verwendung und zum Verständnis der Schrift bei Paulus*. Tübingen: J. C. B. Mohr, 1986.

Kümmel, Werner Georg. *Introduction to the New Testament*. Nashville: Abingdon, 1966.

_____. *The New Testament: The History of the Investigation of its Problems*. New York: Abingdon, 1972.

Lagrange, Marie-Joseph. *Évangile selon Saint Marc*. Paris: J. Gabalda, 1929.

_____. *Évangile selon Saint Matthieu*. 4th ed.; Paris: J. Gabalda, 1927.

Luz, Ulrich. *Matthew 1–7: A Commentary*. Minneapolis: Augsburg, 1989.

Mann, C. S. *Mark: A New Translation with Introduction and Commentary*. Garden City, New York: Doubleday, 1986.

Massebieau, Eugène. *Examen des citations de l'Ancien Testament dans l'Évangile selon Matthieu*. Paris: Fischbacher, 1885.

McCasland, S. "Matthew Twists the Scriptures," *JBL* 80 (1961) 143–148.

Metzger, B. M. "The Formulas Introducing Quotations of Scripture in the New Testament and the Midrash," *JBL* 70 (1951) 297–307.

_____. *The Text of the New Testament: Its Transmission, Corruption, and Restoration* . 2nd ed.; Oxford: Clarendon, 1968.

_____. *A Textual Commentary on the Greek New Testament* . 2nd ed.; New York: United Bible Societies, 1975.

Meyer, Ben F. *The Aims of Jesus* . London: SCM, 1979.

Morgenthaler, Robert. *Statistik des neutestamentlichen Wortschatzes* . Zürich: Gotthelf-Verlag, 1958.

Moule, C. F. D. "Fulfilment-Words in the New Testament: Use and Abuse," *NTS* 14 (1967–1968) 293–320.

Neill, Stephen. *The Interpretation of the New Testament, 1861–1961* . London: Oxford University Press, 1964.

New, David S. "The Confusion of ℸ — ℸ and ℸ, with Special Reference to 1QIsa[a] 29:13," forthcoming in *Revue de Qumrân* .

_____. "The Injunctive Future and Existential Injunctions in the New Testament," *Journal for the Study of the New Testament* 44 (1991) 113–127.

_____. "The Occurrence of αὐτῶν in Matthew 13.15 and the Process of Text Assimilation," *NTS* 37 (1991) 478–480.

Noja, Sergio. "The Samareitikon," in Alan D. Crown, *The Samaritans* (Tübingen: Mohr, 1989) 408–412.

Orchard, Bernard and Harold Riley. *The Order of the Synoptics: Why Three Synoptic Gospels?* Macon, Georgia: Mercer University Press, 1987.

_____ and Thomas R. W. Longstaff, ed. *J. J. Griesbach: Synoptic and Text-critical Studies, 1776–1976* . Cambridge: Cambridge University Press, 1978.

O'Rourke, J. J. "Explicit Old Testament Citations in the Gospels," *Studia Montis Regii* 7 (1964) 37–60.

_____. "The Fulfillment Texts in Matthew," *CBQ* 24 (1962) 394–403.

Ottley, R. R. *The Book of Isaiah According to the Septuagint (Codex Alexandrinus)* ; vol. 2: *Text and Notes* . Cambridge: Cambridge University Press, 1906.

Pesch, Rudolf. "Eine alttestamentliche Ausführungsformel im Matthäus-Evangelium," *BZ* n.s.10 (1966) 221–245; n.s.11 (1967) 79–95.

_____. "Der Gottessohn im matthäischen Evangelienprolog (Mt 1–2): Beobachtungen zu den Zitationsformeln der Reflexionszitate," *Bib* 48 (1967) 395–420.

_____. *Das Marcusevangelium* . 2 vols. Freiburg: Herder, 1977.

Pietersma, Albert. *Two Manuscripts of the Greek Psalter* . Rome: Biblical Institute Press, 1978.

Plummer, Alfred. *A Critical and Exegetical Commentary on the Gospel According to S. Luke* . 5th ed.; Edinburgh: T. & T. Clark, 1922.

Reicke, Bo. "From Strauss to Holtzmann and Meijboom," *NovT* 29 (1987) 1–21.

_____. *The Roots of the Synoptic Gospels* . Philadelphia: Fortress, 1986.

Roberts, Bleddyn Jones. *The Old Testament Text and Versions: The Hebrew Text in Transmission and the History of the Ancient Versions* . Cardiff: University of Wales Press, 1951.

_____. "The Textual Transmission of the Old Testament (including modern critical editions of the Hebrew Bible)," in G. W. Anderson, ed., *Tradition and Interpretation: Essays by Members of the Society for Old Testament Study* (Oxford: Clarendon, 1979).

Robinson, John Arthur Thomas. *Redating the New Testament* . London: SCM, 1976.

Rothfuchs, Wilhelm. *Die Erfüllungszitate des Matthäus-Evangeliums*. Stuttgart: W. Kohlhammer, 1969.

Sanday, William, ed. *Studies in the Synoptic Problem* . Oxford: Clarendon, 1911.

Sanders, E. P. *The Tendencies of the Synoptic Tradition* . London: Cambridge University Press, 1969.

Seeligmann, Isac Leo. *The Septuagint Version of Isaiah: A Discussion of its Problems* . Leiden: E. J. Brill, 1948.

Smith, D. Moody, Jr. "The Use of the Old Testament in the New," in James M. Efird, ed., *The Use of the Old Testament in the New and Other Essays: Studies in Honor of William Franklin Stinespring* (Durham, North Carolina: Duke University Press, 1972).

Soares Prabhu, George M. *The Formula Quotations in the Infancy Narrative of Matthew: An Enquiry into the Tradition History of Mt 1–2* . Rome: Biblical Institute Press, 1976.

Stanton, Graham. "Matthew," in D. A. Carson and H. G. M. Williamson, ed., *It is Written: Scripture Citing Scripture* (Cambridge: Cambridge University Press, 1988) 205–219.

_____. "The Origin and Purpose of Matthew's Gospel: Matthean Scholarship from 1945 to 1980," in Wolfgang Haase, ed., *Aufstieg und Niedergang der Römischen Welt* , vol. 2. pt. 25. sect. 3 (Berlin: Walter de Gruyter, 1985) 1889–1951.

Stendahl, Krister. *The School of St. Matthew and its Use of the Old Testament* . 2nd ed.; Lund: Gleerup, 1968.

Stephenson, T. "The Old Testament Quotations Peculiar to Matthew," *JTS* 20 (1918–1919) 227–229.

Strecker, Georg. *Der Weg der Gerichtigkeit: Untersuchung zur Theologie des Matthäus* . Göttingen: Vandenhoeck & Ruprecht, 1971.

Streeter, Burnett Hillman. *The Four Gospels: A Study of Origins* . London: Macmillan, 1924.

Suhl, Alfred. *Die Funktion der alttestamentlichen Zitate und Anspielungen im Marcusevangelium* . Gütersloh: G. Mohn, 1965.

Sundberg, Albert C, Jr. *The Old Testament of the Early Church* . Cambridge: Harvard University Press, 1964.

Swete, Henry Barclay. *An Introduction to the Old Testament in Greek* . Revised by R. R. Ottley. Cambridge: Cambridge University Press, 1902; repr. New York: KTAV, 1968.

Tholuck, August. *Das Alte Testament im Neuen Testament: über die Citate des Alten Testaments im Neuen Testament und über den Opfer- und Priesterbegriff im Alten und Neuen Testament* . Gotha: Friedrich Perthes, 1972.

Thomas, Kenneth J. "Torah Citations in the Synoptics," *NTS* 24 (1977) 85–96.

Torrey, Charles Cutler. "The Biblical Quotations in Matthew," in Torrey, *Documents of the Primitive Church* (New York: Harper & Bros., 1941) 41–90.

Toy, Crawford Howell.*The Old Testament Quotations in the New Testament.* New York, 1884.

Tuckett, C. M. "The Griesbach Hypothesis in the 19th Century," *Journal for the Study of the New Testament* 3 (1979) 48–60.

_____. *The Revival of the Griesbach Hypothesis: An Analysis and Appraisal.* Cambridge: Cambridge University Press, 1983.

van Cangh, J. M. "La Bible de Matthieu: Les citations d'accomplissement," *ETL* 6 (1975) 205–211.

van Segbroeck, F. "Les citations d'accomplissement dans l'Évangile selon saint Matthieu d'après trois ouvrages récents," in M. Didier, ed., *L'Évangile selon Matthieu: Rédaction et théologie* (Gembloux: J. Duculot, 1972) 107–130.

_____. "Le scandale de l'incroyance: La signification de Mt. XIII, 35," *ETL* 41 (1965) 344–372.

Venard, A. "Citations," *DBSup* 2 (1934) col. 24.

Weisse Christian Hermann. *Die evangelische Geschichte kritisch und philosophisch bearbeitet* ; vol. 1 (Leipzig: Breitkopf und Härtel, 1838).

Westermann, C. "Prophetenzitate im Neuen Testament," *EvT* 27 (1967) 307–317.

Wevers, John William. *Text History of the Greek Deuteronomy* . Göttingen: Vandenhoeck & Ruprecht, 1978.

_____. *Text History of the Greek Genesis* . Göttingen: Vandenhoeck & Ruprecht, 1974.

_____.*Text History of the Greek Numbers* . Göttingen: Vandenhoeck & Ruprecht, 1982.

Wilcox, Max. "Text Form," in D. A. Carson and H. G. M. Williamson, ed., *It is Written: Scripture Citing Scripture* (Cambridge: Cambridge University Press, 1988) 193–204.

Wilke, Christian Gottlob. *Der Urevangelist oder exegetisch kritische Untersuchung über das Verwandtschaftsverhältniss der drei ersten Evangelien* . Dresden and Leipzig: G. Fleischer, 1838.

Woods, F. H. "The Origin and Mutual Relation of the Synoptic Gospels," in William Sanday, ed., *Studia Biblica et Ecclesiastica: Essays Chiefly in Biblical and Patristic Criticism* ; vol. 2 (Oxford, 1890) 59–104.

Würthwein, Ernst. *The Text of the Old Testament: An Introduction to the Biblia Hebraica* . Grand Rapids: Eerdmans, 1979.

lectio difficilior 98n
liturgical/catechetical
 texts 71, 74, 75, 76, 79,
 97, 98, 109n
Logia 12, 25n
Marcan priority 1, 14
Matthean style 68n, 84,
 109
midrash pesher 27
Mishnah 31n
Nash Papyrus 74, 75, 76
orthographical
 differences 52
papyrus-963 58, 74n, 79
Pauline epistles,
 quotations in the 122
Peschitta 32
preferred text 39
"Q" 1, 6, 25, 25n, 30,
 46n, 55n, 56, 59, 64, 80,
 117, 118, 119
Qumran, texts from 24,
 27, 31n, 65n, 97
 Habbakuk Commentary
 (DSH) 27, 27n, 28
1QIsa^a 65n
quotation, definition of
 9, 74, 89-90, 96-97
rabbinic tradition 112n
Reflexionscitate 7, 16n,
 17, 19, 22, 24, 31, 34, 35
scribal assimilation
 49, 83
synoptic problem
 defined 1;
 history of 1-3;
 current interest in 4
targumization 25, 122
Targums 25, 25n, 33
testimonies 103n, 122
text-types 7-8, 23, 24n,
 32, 34-37, 120
Tübingen school 2, 3
two-document hypothesis
 defined 1;
 as presupposition 30n,
 73
 and historicity 2-4;
 and quotations 34, 37,
 121;

and form criticism 5,
 75;
and redaction criticism
 5-6;
and source criticism 6;
and text criticism
 6, 73-74
Urmarcus 7, 11-14, 15n, 67n

Printed in the United States
1052800001B/96

9 781555 409210